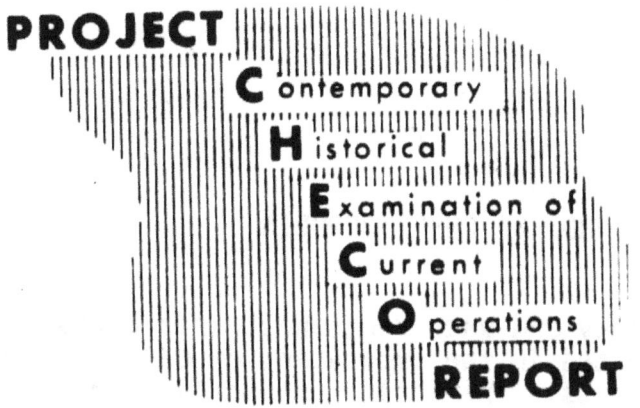

PROJECT
Contemporary
Historical
Examination of
Current
Operations
REPORT

VIETNAMIZATION OF THE AIR WAR, 1970 - 1971

8 OCTOBER 1971

HQ PACAF

Directorate of Operations Analysis
CHECO/CORONA HARVEST DIVISION

Prepared by:

CAPT DRUE L. DEBERRY

Project CHECO 7th AF, DOAC

PROJECT CHECO REPORTS

The counterinsurgency and unconventional warfare environment of Southeast Asia has resulted in the employment of USAF airpower to meet a multitude of requirements. The varied applications of airpower have involved the full spectrum of USAF aerospace vehicles, support equipment, and manpower. As a result, there has been an accumulation of operational data and experiences that, as a priority, must be collected, documented, and analyzed as to current and future impact upon USAF policies, concepts, and doctrine.

Fortunately, the value of collecting and documenting our SEA experiences was recognized at an early date. In 1962, Hq USAF directed CINCPACAF to establish an activity that would be primarily responsive to Air Staff requirements and direction, and would provide timely and analytical studies of USAF combat operations in SEA.

Project CHECO, an acronym for Contemporary Historical Examination of Current Operations, was established to meet this Air Staff requirement. Managed by Hq PACAF, with elements at Hq 7AF and 7AF/13AF, Project CHECO provides a scholarly, "on-going" historical examination, documentation, and reporting on USAF policies, concepts, and doctrine in PACOM. This CHECO report is part of the overall documentation and examination which is being accomplished. It is an authentic source for an assessment of the effectiveness of USAF airpower in PACOM when used in proper context. The reader must view the study in relation to the events and circumstances at the time of its preparation--recognizing that it was prepared on a contemporary basis which restricted perspective and that the author's research was limited to records available within his local headquarters area.

ERNEST C. HARDIN, JR., Major General, USAF
Chief of Staff

REPLY TO
ATTN OF: DOAD

8 October 1971

SUBJECT: Project CHECO Report, "Vietnamization of the Air War, 1970-1971" (U)

TO: SEE DISTRIBUTION PAGE

1. Attached is a SECRET NOFORN document. It shall be transported, stored, safeguarded, and accounted for in accordance with applicable security directives. SPECIAL HANDLING REQUIRED, NOT RELEASABLE TO FOREIGN NATIONALS. The information contained in this document will not be disclosed to foreign nations or their representatives. Retain or destroy in accordance with AFR 205-1. Do not return.

2. This letter does not contain classified information and may be declassified if attachment is removed from it.

FOR THE COMMANDER IN CHIEF

MIKE DELEON, Colonel, USAF
Chief, CHECO/CORONA HARVEST Division
Directorate of Operations Analysis
DCS/Operations

1 Atch
Proj CHECO Rprt (S/NF),
8 Oct 71

DISTRIBUTION LIST

1. SECRETARY OF THE AIR FORCE

    a. SAFAA 1
    b. SAFLL 1
    c. SAFOI 2
    d. SAFUS 1

2. HEADQUARTERS USAF

    a. AFNB 1

    b. AFCCS
        (1) AFCCSSA 1
        (2) AFCVC 1
        (3) AFCAV 1
        (4) AFCHO 2

    c. AFCSA
        (1) AFCSAG 1
        (2) AFCSAMI 1

    d. SAJ 1

    e. AFIGO
        (1) OSIIAP 3
        (2) IGS 1

    f. AFSG 1

    g. AFINATC 5

    h. AFAAC 1
        (1) AFACMI 1

    i. AFODC
        (1) AFPRC 1
        (2) AFPRE 1
        (3) AFPRM 1

    j. AFPDC
        (1) AFDPW 1

    k. AFRD
        (1) AFRDP 1
        (2) AFRDQ 1
        (3) AFRDQPC 1
        (4) AFRDR 1
        (5) AFRDQL 1

    l. AFSDC
        (1) AFSLP 1
        (2) AFSME 1
        (3) AFSMS 1
        (4) AFSSS 1
        (5) AFSTP 1

    m. AFTAC 1

    n. AFXO 1
        (1) AFXOB 1
        (2) AFXOD 1
        (3) AFXODC 1
        (4) AFXODD 1
        (5) AFXODL 1
        (6) AFXOOG 1
        (7) AFXOSL 1
        (8) AFXOOSN 1
        (9) AFXOOSO 1
        (10) AFXOOSS 1
        (11) AFXOOSV 1
        (12) AFXOOTR 1
        (13) AFXOOTW 1
        (14) AFXOOTZ 1
        (15) AF/XOX 6
        (16) AFXOXXG 1

3. MAJOR COMMAND

   a. TAC

      (1) HEADQUARTERS
          (a) DO. 1
          (b) XP. 1
          (c) DOCC. 1
          (d) DREA. 1
          (e) IN. 1

      (2) AIR FORCES
          (a) 12AF
              1. DOO. 1
              2. IN 1
          (b) T9AF(IN). 1
          (c) USAFSOF(DO) 1

      (3) WINGS
          (a) 1SOW(DOI) 1
          (b) 23TFW(DOI). 1
          (c) 27TRW(DOI). 1
          (d) 33TFW(DOI). 1
          (e) 64TAW(DOI). 1
          (f) 67TRW(DOI). 1
          (g) 75TRW(DOI). 1
          (h) 316TAW(DOX) 1
          (i) 363TRW(DOI) 1
          (j) 464TFW(DOI) 1
          (k) 474TFW(DOI) 1
          (l) 479TFW(DOI) 1
          (m) 516TAW(DOX) 1
          (n) 4403TFW(DOI). 1
          (o) 58TAC FTR TNG WG. . 1
          (p) 354TFW(DOI) 1
          (q) 60MAWG(DOOXI) . . . 1

      (4) TAC CENTERS, SCHOOLS
          (a) USAFTAWC(DRA) . . . 1
          (b) USAFTFWC(DRA) . . . 1
          (c) USAFAGOS(EDA) . . . 1

   b. SAC

      (1) HEADQUARTERS
          (a) DOX 1
          (b) XPX 1
          (c) DM. 1
          (d) IN. 1
          (e) NR. 1
          (f) HO. 1

      (2) AIR FORCES
          (a) 2AF(INCS) 1
          (b) 8AF(DOA). 2
          (c) 15AF(INCE). 1

   c. MAC

      (1) HEADQUARTERS
          (a) DOI 1
          (b) DOO 1
          (c) CSEH. 1
          (d) MACOA 1

      (2) MAC SERVICES
          (a) AWS(HO) 1
          (b) ARRS(XP). 1
          (c) ACGS(CGO) 1

   d. ADC

      (1) HEADQUARTERS
          (a) DO. 1
          (b) DOT 1
          (c) XPC 1

      (2) AIR DIVISIONS
          (a) 25AD(DOI) 1
          (b) 23AD(DOI) 1
          (c) 20AD(DOI) 1

   e. ATC
      (1) DOSPI 1

f. AFLC

   (1) HEADQUARTERS
      (a) XOX 1

g. AFSC

   (1) HEADQUARTERS
      (a) XRP 1
      (b) XRLW. 1
      (c) SAMSO(XRS). 1
      (d) SDA 1
      (e) CSH 1
      (f) ASD(RWST) 1
      (g) ESD(XR) 1
      (h) RADC(DOTL). 1
      (i) ADTC(CCN) 1
      (j) ADTC(SSLT). 1
      (k) ESD(YW) 1
      (l) AFATL(DL) 1

h. USAFSS

   (1) HEADQUARTERS
      (a) AFSCC(SUR). 2

   (2) SUBORDINATE UNITS
      (a) Eur Scty Rgn(OPD-P) . 1
      (b) 6940 Scty Wg(OOD) . . 1

i. AAC

   (1) HEADQUARTERS
      (a) ALDOC-A 1

j. USAFSO

   (1) HEADQUARTERS
      (a) CSH 1

k. PACAF

   (1) HEADQUARTERS
      (a) DP 1
      (b) IN 1
      (c) XP 2
      (d) CSH. 1
      (e) DOAD 6
      (f) DC 1
      (g) DM 1

   (2) AIR FORCES
      (a) 5AF
         1. CSH 1
         2. XP. 1
         3. DO. 1
      (b) Det 8, ASD(DOASD). . 1
      (c) 7AF
         1. DO. 1
         2. IN. 1
         3. XP. 1
         4. DOCT. 1
         5. DOAC. 2
      (d) 13AF
         1. CSH 1
      (e) 7/13AF(CHECO). . . . 1

   (3) AIR DIVISIONS
      (a) 313AD(DOI) 1
      (b) 314AD(XOP) 2
      (c) 327AD
         1. IN. 1
      (d) 834AD(DO). 2

(4) WINGS
    (a) 8TFW(DOEA) 1
    (b) 12TFW(DOIN). 1
    (c) 56SOW)WHD) 1
    (d) 366TFW(DO) 1
    (e) 388TFWI(DO). 1
    (f) 405TFW(DOEA) 1
    (g) 432TRW(DOI). 1
    (h) 483TAC ALFT WG 1
    (i) 475TFW(DCO). 1
    (j) 1st Test Sq(A) 1

(5) OTHER UNITS
    (a) Task Force ALPHA (IN). . 1
    (b) 504TASG(DO). 1
    (c) Air Force Advisory Gp. . 1

1. USAFE

(1) HEADQUARTERS
    (a) DOA. 1
    (b) DOLO 1
    (c) DOO. 1
    (d) XDC. 1

(2) AIR FORCES
    (a) 3AF(DO). 2
    (b) 16AF(DO) 1
    (c) 17AF(IN) 1

(3) WINGS
    (a) 36TFW(DCOID) 1
    (b) 50TFW(DOA) 1
    (c) 20TFW(DOI) 1
    (d) 401TFW(DCOI) 1
    (e) 513TAW(DOI). 1

4. SEPARATE OPERATING AGENCIES
  a. ACIC(DOP). 2
  b. AFRES(XP). 2
  c. AU
    1. ACSC-SA 1
    2. AUL(SE)-69-108. 2
    3. ASI(ASD-1). 1
    4. ASI(HOA). 2
  d. ANALYTIC SERVICES, INC . 1
  e. USAFA
    1. DFH 1
  f. AFAG(THAILAND) 1

5. MILITARY DEPARTMENTS, UNIFIED AND SPECIFIED COMMANDS, AND JOINT STAFFS

    a. COMUSJAPAN 1
    b. CINCPAC (SAG) 1
    c. CINCPAC (J301) 1
    d. CINCPACFLT (Code 321) 1
    e. COMUSKOREA (ATTN: J-3) 1
    f. COMUSMACTHAI 1
    g. COMUSMACV (TSCO) 1
    h. COMUSTDC (J3) 1
    i. USCINCEUR (ECJB) 1
    j. USCINCSO (DCC) 1
    k. CINCLANT (N31) 1
    l. CHIEF, NAVAL OPERATIONS 1
    m. COMMANDANT, MARINE CORPS (ABQ) 1
    n. CINCONAD (CHSV-M) 1
    o. DEPARTMENT OF THE ARMY (TAGO) 1
    p. JOINT CHIEFS OF STAFF (J3RR&A) 1
    q. JSTPS 1
    r. SECRETARY OF DEFENSE (OASD/SA) 1
    s. CINCSTRIKE (STRJ-3) 1
    t. CINCAL (HIST) 1
    u. MAAG-CHINA/AF Section (MGAF-O) 1
    v. HQ ALLIED FORCES NORTHERN EUROPE (U.S. DOCUMENTS OFFICE) 1
    w. USMACV (MACJ031) 1

6. SCHOOLS

    a. Senior USAF Representative, National War College 1
    b. Senior USAF Representative, Armed Forces Staff College 1
    c. Senior USAF Rep, Industrial College of the Armed Forces 1
    d. Senior USAF Representative, Naval Amphibious School 1
    e. Senior USAF Rep, U.S. Marine Corps Education Center 1
    f. Senior USAF Representative, U.S. Naval War College 1
    g. Senior USAF Representative, U.S. Army War College 1
    h. Senior USAF Rep, U.S. Army C&G Staff College 1
    i. Senior USAF Representative, U.S. Army Infantry School 1
    j. Senior USAF Rep, U.S. Army JFK Center for Special Warfare ... 1
    k. Senior USAF Representative, U.S. Army Field Artillery School 1
    l. Senior USAF Representative, U.S. Liaison Office 1

7. SPECIAL

    a. The RAND Corporation 1
    b. U.S. Air Attache, Vientiane 1

	Page
CHAPTER VIII - GUNSHIPS	46
Expansion	46
Interdiction	48
Summary	49
CHAPTER IX - AIRLIFT	50
Expansion	50
Training	51
Performance	53
CHAPTER X - RECONNAISSANCE AND PSYCHOLOGICAL WARFARE	55
Reconnaissance	55
Airborne Radio Direction Finding	56
Psychological Warfare	57
CHAPTER XI - AIR LOGISTICS	59
CHAPTER XII - FACILITIES	66
CHAPTER XIII - SUMMING UP	70
APPENDIX	
I. VNAF FORCE PROGRAM	74
II. MOBILE TRAINING TEAMS	75
III. INTEGRATED TRAINING PROGRAM	80
IV. VNAF GROWTH, JANUARY 1970-JUNE 1971	82
FOOTNOTES	
Chapter I	89
Chapter II	89
Chapter III	90
Chapter IV	91
Chapter V	93
Chapter VI	94
Chapter VII	95
Chapter VIII	95
Chapter IX	96
Chapter X	96
Chapter XI	97
Chapter XII	98
Chapter XIII	99
GLOSSARY	100

TABLE OF CONTENTS

	Page
FOREWORD	xiv
CHAPTER I - BACKGROUND	1
CHAPTER II - THE IMPROVEMENT AND MODERNIZATION PROGRAM	4
Program I	4
Program II	4
Program III	5
Restructuring	7
Trends	8
CHAPTER III - TRAINING	11
Pacer Bravo and Pacer Enhance	13
Mobile Training Teams	16
Air Training Center	16
Integrated Training	18
VNAF On-the-Job Training	19
Observations	20
CHAPTER IV - OPERATIONS	21
Cambodia	22
Laos	24
Conclusion	27
CHAPTER V - TACTICAL AIR CONTROL SYSTEM	28
Air Operations Command	28
Tactical Air Control Center	30
Direct Air Support Centers	30
Immediate Request Net	31
Air Liaison Officers and Forward Air Controllers	32
Airlift Control Center	33
Air Control and Warning	34
CHAPTER VI - HELICOPTERS	36
Doctrine	37
Personnel	39
CHAPTER VII - FIGHTERS	41
Performance	41
Limited Expansion	43
Expanded Operational Capability	44

ABOUT THE AUTHOR

Captain Drue L. DeBerry is a senior navigator with 3,500 hours flying time in C-135 and C-141 transports and AC-130 gunships. He served one tour in Southeast Asia. He graduated from the United States Air Force Academy in 1963. In 1970, he graduated from the University of Oklahoma with a M.A. in History. In 1970, he published "Gold Rush California: The Roots of a Regional Ethos," in the Pacific Historian.

LIST OF FIGURES

FIGURE		Follows Page
1.	VNAF Organizational Chart	8
2.	Location of the VNAF Air Divisions	8
3.	Pacer Bravo Courses	14
4.	Pacer Bravo: A Member of a USAF Mobile Training Team Watches a Former Student Conduct Instruction on Aircraft Landing Gear Systems at Nha Trang AB, South Vietnam	14
5.	Pacer Bravo Training Aid: Aircraft Engine	14
6.	Pacer Bravo Training Aid: Hydraulic System Mockup	14
7.	UH-1 Job Performance Aid	16
8.	Colonel Oanh, Commander of the VNAF Air Training Center at Nha Trang AB Prepares for a Flight in the First Aircraft Built in South Vietnam, The TP-1	16
9.	Integrated Training: VNAF Airmen Work Side-by-Side with United States Army Personnel of the 205th Aviation Company	18
10.	VNAF A-1 on a Bombing Mission	22
11.	Percent of Fighter and Fixed-Wing Gunship Attack Sorties Flown by VNAF in the RVN and Cambodia	28
12.	VNAF Tactical Air Control Center	28
13.	Tactical Air Support Immediate Net	28
14.	Tactical Air Support Operations	32
15.	VNAF O-1 Forward Air Controller Marking a Target	32
16.	Tactical Air Support, Preplanned Airlift	34
17.	USAF Attack Sorties and VNAF Strike Sorties, Republic of Vietnam, 1970-1971	42

FIGURE	Follows Page
18. VNAF Airmen Loading Bombs on an A-37	44
19. VNAF F-5 Fighter	44
20. USAF and VNAF Gunship Sorties, Republic of Vietnam, 1970-1971	46
21. AC-119 Gunship	48
22. C-7 Transport	52
23. Airlift Support of RVNAF	54
24. VNAF Transport Sorties	54
25. Integrated Training at the 12th Reconnaissance Intelligence Technical Squadron	56
26. One Member of a USAF Mobile Training Team at the VNAF Air Logistics Center Giving Instruction and Assistance	60
27. Hard Core Facility Transfer Summary, 30 June 1971	66
28. VNAF Family Housing under Construction	68
29. The Vietnamization of the Air War	70

FOREWORD

This report describes the improvement and modernization of the Vietnamese Air Force (VNAF) from January 1970 to July 1971. The growth and development of the VNAF during this period was an integral part of the Consolidated Republic of Vietnam Improvement and Modernization Program (CRIMP). The goal of CRIMP was to assure the self-sufficiency of the Republic of Vietnam Armed Forces (RVNAF) after the withdrawal of United States combat forces.

Self-sufficiency in this context implied that the armed forces of the Government of Vietnam (GVN) could maintain the level of security that had been won jointly by the United States and South Vietnam. This did not mean that United States assistance would no longer be required to protect South Vietnamese independence. South Vietnam did not possess or plan to develop the industrial capacity to produce the equipment necessary for defense. The United States would continue to provide the materiel support for the defense of South Vietnam, as well as a military team to advise the RVNAF--but the RVNAF would have the capability of effectively using that equipment to maintain the security of South Vietnam without the active armed assistance of United States military forces. Though the United States advisory effort would still be needed, the United States would no longer be required to bear arms in defense of South Vietnam. That is the meaning of the term "self-sufficiency" as it is used in this report.

The history of the VNAF from its inception to early 1970 was traced in two previous CHECO Reports: The Organization, Mission and Growth of the Vietnamese Air Force, 1949-1968; and the VNAF Improvement and Modernization Program [1968-1970]. Therefore only the briefest summary of that history will be given here. The emphasis of the present report will be on the efforts of the United States Air Force (USAF) to improve and expand VNAF capability during the eighteen month period ending in July 1971. The chapters of this report deal with mission functions--"Airlift," for example, or "Logistics,"--and describe the broad outlines of the entire VNAF.

A companion volume to this report, The VNAF Air Divisions: Reports on Improvement and Modernization, describes the effects of CRIMP on each of the VNAF air divisions. Each chapter of The VNAF Air Divisions was written by a different author and the report thus reflects five independent efforts to examine the results of CRIMP at the unit level.

Together, these two volumes describe the VNAF as it developed between January 1970 and July 1971.

CHAPTER I

BACKGROUND

In 1954 one auxiliary squadron of the French Air Force in Indochina was manned by Vietnamese. When it separated from the French Air Force in 1955, this small force became the nucleus of the VNAF. It consisted of thirty-two C-47 transports and a few Morane-Saulnier observation planes.[1]

French advisors were withdrawn from Vietnam in 1956 and succeeded by Americans. At that time there were only 92 pilots in the VNAF.[2]

The most conspicuous change in the VNAF between 1956 and 1962 was its growth and diversification. Between 1956 and 1962 the number of personnel increased from a few hundred to 5,700 and the aircraft inventory increased to some 140 and included A-1s, T-28s, C-47s, H-19s, and H-34s.[3]

The USAF assumed an active flying mission in South Vietnam in 1961 when a small number of USAF pilots began flying tactical missions with the VNAF. USAF participation grew until by the mid-1960s it eclipsed the VNAF role almost entirely.[4] There were a few senior USAF officers who opposed this trend and who believed it would be more productive to improve the VNAF rather than have the USAF assume the responsibility for the air war. But circumstances seemed compelling and the decisions made between 1965 and 1968 progressively increased USAF dominance of air-operations--a process which had to be reversed afterwards.[5]

The VNAF did not stagnate between 1961 and 1968. By the time the decision was made in 1968 to re-Vietnamize the war, the VNAF had expanded some and had assumed more diversified missions. By then there were 20 VNAF squadrons and several newer types of aircraft.

Planning assumptions for further VNAF expansion included an eventual American withdrawal. But before that withdrawal could be accomplished, existing VNAF weaknesses had to be corrected, the force had to be more than doubled in size and reorganized to accommodate the expansion, and a massive training program had to be developed and implemented by the USAF and VNAF. [6/]

In 1969 American defense officials in both Washington and Vietnam gave Vietnamization a priority equal to the actual combat mission of Allied forces. At the same time, a senior USAF advisor did not hesitate to characterize the program for the VNAF as a "mammoth task."

The expansion and modernization of the Army of the Republic of Vietnam (ARVN) was begun in 1967 but the parallel VNAF program did not start until a year later. In 1969 the chief of the Air Force Advisory Group in Vietnam, Brigadier General Charles W. Carson, Jr., commented that the VNAF: [7/]

> . . . with the longest lead-time training requirements, was just beginning a program that would not be completed until two years after achievement of the ARVN force goals. A 1967 program, which would have not only resulted in a more effective military force, but also would have achieved the goal at an earlier date than now possible.

By late 1969 the VNAF had grown from a small auxiliary squadron of the French Air Force to a considerably larger force, but one not yet capable of independently fighting the air war in South Vietnam. It was the goal of both the USAF and the VNAF in late 1969 to develop a self-sufficient Vietnamese Air Force. When the VNAF could fly and maintain their airplanes without the direct assistance of USAF personnel, Vietnamization of the air war would be a reality.

CHAPTER II

THE IMPROVEMENT AND MODERNIZATION PROGRAM

The term "Vietnamization" was first used by President Nixon on 3 November 1969 when he said, "In the previous administration, we Americanized the war; in this administration, we are Vietnamizing the search for peace." The basic guidelines and plans for the Vietnamization program were drawn up in 1968 and 1969 as an alternative to a continued United States combat role in the war.[8] For Vietnamization to succeed, RVNAF capability had to be improved and modernized.

Program I

The Improvement and Modernization (I&M) program for the VNAF occurred in several phases. Program I, conceived in early 1968, was based on the assumption that USAF participation in the war would remain at the early 1968 level. Under this program, four of the VNAF's five H-34 helicopter squadrons were designated for conversion to UH-1s and four more UH-1 squadrons were scheduled additions to bring the total VNAF rotary and fixed wing force to 24.[9] It was a modest program intended to strengthen the RVNAF at a time when one of the options also being considered by the Commander of the Military Assistance Command, Vietnam (MACV), the Joint Chiefs of Staff (JCS), and President Johnson was to continue strengthening United States forces in Vietnam.

Program II

Within two months, however, the idea of making the RVNAF strong enough to fight independently became dominant. The assumption was made that a mutual United States and North Vietnamese withdrawal would occur, and that a residual threat composed of indigenous Viet Cong supported by some North Vietnamese cadres would remain. This assumption led to Program II which was at first considered either an alternative to Program I or a program to be undertaken after the completion of Program I. Program II plans called for an increase in the total force to 39 squadrons. Authorized personnel strength increased from approximately 17,000 to 36,000 men.

Originally, MACV believed that five years would be necessary to accomplish Program II, but in April 1969 the Secretary of Defense directed that the schedule be accelerated and completed by December 1971.[10/] Because of this accelerated schedule Program II was renamed Program II-A. Vietnamese unit activations were completed early wherever possible. The VNAF activated one liaison squadron in the third quarter of Fiscal Year (FY) 70 rather than in the fourth quarter of FY 71 as originally planned. The first CH-47 Chinook helicopter squadron was activated six months earlier than planned; three fighter squadrons were activated in late 1970, nine months early; and three transport squadrons were consolidated into two, one activating five months early, the other three months early. This Program II-A force was planned to include 39 squadrons.[11/] In late 1969, however, the Secretary of Defense directed further planning for making the RVNAF even stronger.[12/]

Program III

The I&M Program as it was planned through Program II-A was considered the maximum force attainable with the time and resources available. One top USAF advisor said, "If we give them more than they can support in terms of their economy and available manpower, we might rupture them."[13/] The planners recognized that the force did not correspond to all the needs of the air war and that risks would inhere in the U.S. drawdown. The magnitude of those risks would be determined by the actual enemy threat, the extent of the U.S. drawdown, and the strength of the RVNAF. Thus Program III was planned and implemented to fill remaining deficiencies and provide the VNAF with several added capabilities not included in Programs I and II.[14/]

Program III was designed to correct deficiencies in air defense, reconnaissance, helicopter support for the ARVN, fixed-wing transport, and interdiction. Many of the Program III alterations had to be more than simple add-ons to the force. They had to be qualitative as well as quantitative improvements.

To compensate for the anticipated lack of experienced middle management in the VNAF, the squadrons were enlarged so the same number of officers and NCOs would be responsible for more people and equipment. Also, more units were put onto the existing bases to avoid increasing the number of installations with a consequent increase in base-support units.

Program III proposed a final force of 50 squadrons, 1,300 aircraft, and 52,171 personnel compared to 39 squadrons, 934 aircraft, and 35,786 personnel under Program II-A.[15/] The organizations to be added were selected carefully to expand tactical functions which would contribute most toward finding and destroying the enemy's main force units in the field.

Restructuring

Determining what the VNAF needed to take over the air war was only half the planning picture. Other planning was required so that the VNAF could absorb its new people, equipment, and missions. This required a total restructuring. The established and more-or-less independent wings were to be welded together into five air divisions. The new structure was the usual pyramid of squadrons reporting to wings, wings reporting to divisions, and divisions reporting to a headquarters which had functional directorates. Five numbered air divisions, four corresponding to the four military regions and the fifth located in the Capital Military Region, were established (See Figure 1). All five were activated by 1 January 1971. It is noteworthy that the planning for activation was carried out largely by VNAF planners who demonstrated a maturing capacity in this function.[16/]

In addition to the air divisions, an Air Logistics Command was established at Bien Hoa Air Base (AB) and the training facilities at Nha Trang AB were redesignated as the Air Training Center. The tactical air control system (TACS) and aircraft control and warning (AC&W) systems were also expanded.[17/]

For the 1st Air Division (AD) located in northern South Vietnam at Da Nang AB, VNAF, and AFGP planners put the emphasis on air defense and special air warfare plus improved support for the ARVN. (See Figure 2.) The 2nd AD which was responsible for air support in Military Region (MR) 2, the largest MR in South Vietnam, was composed of two wings each having fighters, liaison aircraft, and helicopters. The 2nd AD had one wing stationed in the Annamite Mountains at Pleiku AB, a region not inhabited by ethnic Vietnamese. The other wing and 2nd AD Headquarters were located at Nha Trang AB.

Bien Hoa AB, 12 miles north of Saigon, was the home of the 3rd AD as well as the VNAF Air Logistics Command (ALC), the computerized supply and maintenance counterpart of the USAF's Air Force Logistics Command (AFLC). The 4th AD was assigned to MR 4, the flat delta region south of Saigon, and located at Binh Thuy AB. Two helicopter squadrons of the 4th AD's 84th Wing were stationed at Soc Trang AB, several miles south of Binh Thuy. It was in MR 4 that the VNAF first assumed control of a Direct Air Support Center (DASC), responsibility for support of the ARVN, and operational control of an airbase (Soc Trang AB). The 4th AD's early thrust to self-sufficiency was closely studied by USAF and VNAF planners for lessons to be applied elsewhere in South Vietnam.[18]

At Tan Son Nhut AB, 5th Air Division headquarters, the transport missions dominated. There were no fighters stationed at the base, but there were gunships, reconnaissance aircraft, and helicopters. VNAF headquarters was also located at Tan Son Nhut AB.

Trends

The trends in 1970 and 1971 planning were: (1) to seek ways to accelerate VNAF self-sufficiency by early activations, (2) to move training from the United States to Vietnam, and (3) to improve the VNAF's equipment.

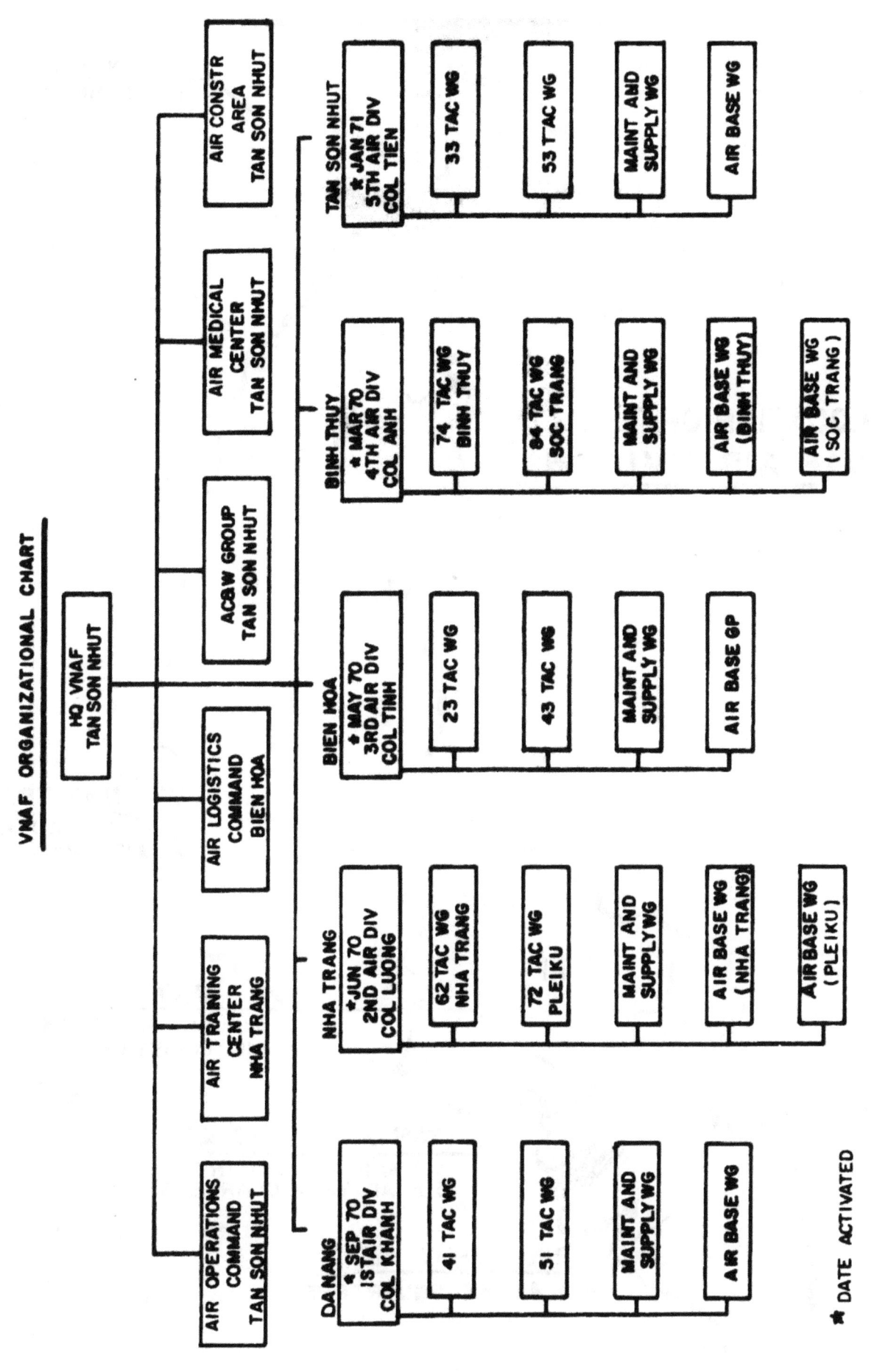

FIGURE 1

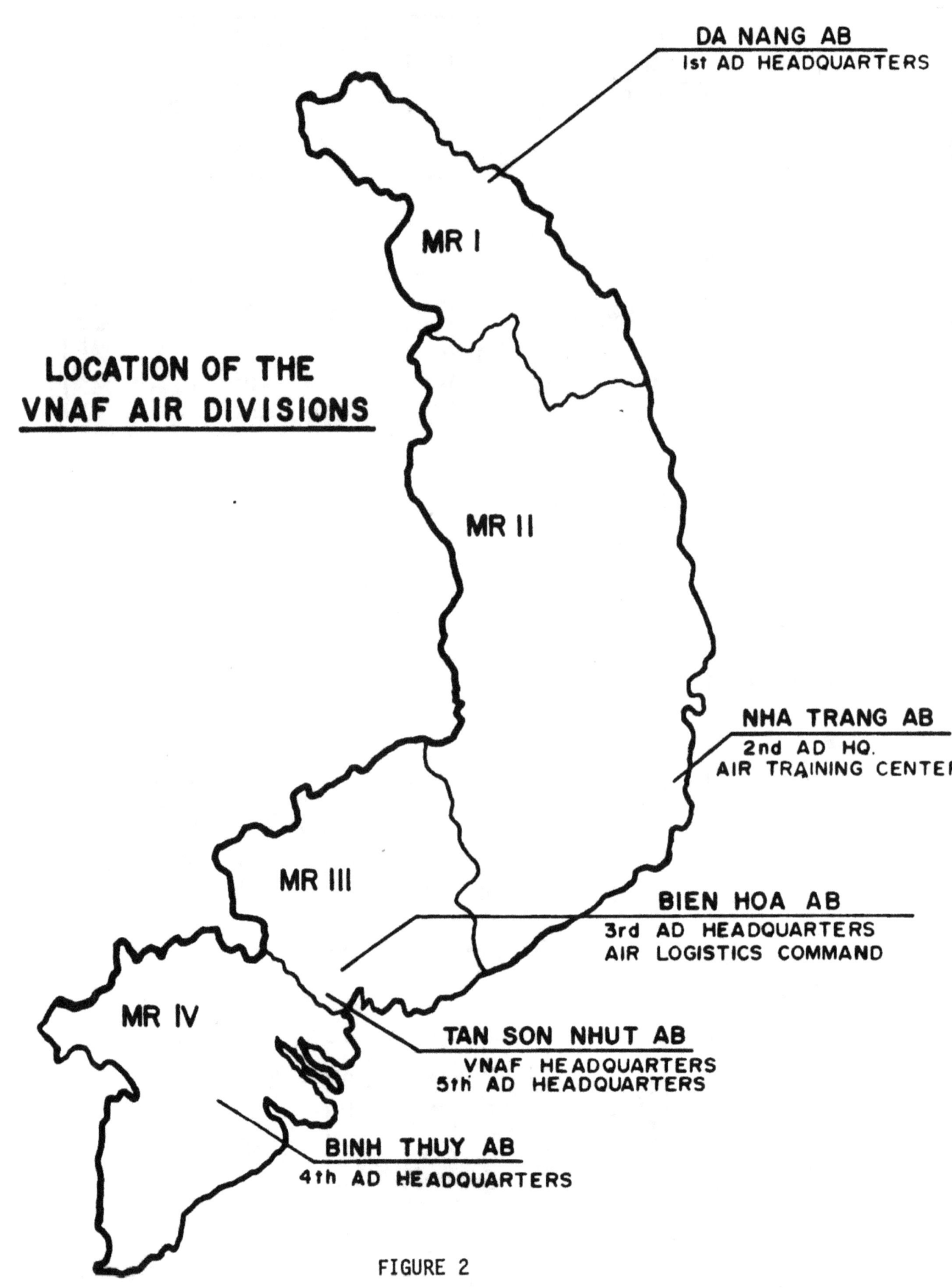

FIGURE 2

Activating the squadrons before their scheduled times seemed impossible during the course of an already accelerated Program II. "We figured the program was so tight, a sneeze would blow it apart," said a former AFGP Chief, Brigadier General Kendall S. Young.[19/] Nevertheless, even those originally tight schedules were exceeded in almost every category.

In another effort to accelerate squadron activations and reduce costs, VNAF C-123 and AC-119 combat crew training was conducted at Phan Rang AB, Vietnam by the USAF 14th Special Operations Wing. VNAF graduates of this course were also trained as instructors and assisted in training succeeding VNAF students. The success of this program bred confidence in in-country training programs and thus contributed to VNAF self-sufficiciency. Other training programs were reviewed to see if they could be moved from the United States to South Vietnam, thereby reducing reliance on United States schools. USAF Mobile Training Teams (MTTs) sent to Vietnam to conduct training gave further evidence of this trend.

Improving VNAF equipment was a continuing concern of USAF advisors. The 819th VNAF squadron was activated in 1971 with AC-119s instead of the AC-47s originally planned. Shorter training time was possible since the C-119G was already in the VNAF inventory. At the same time this substitution freed AC-47s for military assistance programs in Laos, Thailand, and elsewhere. The addition of C-123s and C-7s would enhance VNAF airlift capability substantially by late 1971.[20/] C-7 training, like that for the C-123s and AC-119s, was conducted at Phan Rang AB.

Thus the broad outlines took shape. Emphasis on self-sufficiency for the RVNAF as a whole was evident when a new name, CRIMP (Consolidated Republic of Vietnam Armed Forces Improvement and Modernization Program), was adopted in 1971. Meanwhile, detailed planning continued for improving various mission capabilities.

CHAPTER III
TRAINING

Training was the key to VNAF self-sufficiency; and more than anything else, CRIMP--the largest Military Assistance Program (MAP) in United States history--was a training program. Training had to meet two essential objectives for the VNAF to become self-sufficient: (1) personnel had to be trained to meet the immediate needs of expansion, and (2) the VNAF had to develop the capability to train replacements for personnel lost through attrition.

In terms of sheer numbers of personnel the requirements for expansion far exceeded those of attrition, and it was during the expansion phase that USAF assistance would be most necessary. In January 1970 the authorized strength of the VNAF was 35,786. Of this number, 35,435--90 percent--were assigned, but over 17,000 were unskilled. In March 1971 CRIMP authorized a VNAF strength increase to 52,171. This CRIMP addition of slightly less than 17,000 untrained personnel brought the total training requirement for 1970 and the first six months of 1971 to over 34,000--and this figure included only those personnel who needed training to perform at the lowest skill level.[21] Upgrade training also had to be conducted. Massive United States assistance was necessary to meet these requirements for expansion.

It was in reaching the second essential goal--establishing the VNAF capability to train replacements for attrition losses--that self-sufficiency would stand the acid test. The extent of United States assistance needed to train attrition replacements after the initial expansion requirements were satisfied would provide a subjective measure of VNAF self-sufficiency.

The interrelationship between these two training objectives was not clearly realized during the early stages of CRIMP planning, but that relationship emerged as planning progressed. Previous MAP efforts had focused on teaching foreign students English and then training them in the United States, but because of the cost, language training capacity, time available, and the mass of people involved, it became obvious in late 1969 that it was not feasible to follow this established pattern. Training had to be shifted from the United States to South Vietnam.

The urgency of time prompted the shift of the major MAP training effort to South Vietnam.[22] The increased pace of unit activations directed by Program II-A and the increased total number of units directed by CRIMP required that more people be trained and trained sooner. Before training could be started in the United States, VNAF recruits had to learn English, and the Saigon English Language School--the starting point in the training pipeline to the United States--could not provide ". . . sufficient graduates to meet the quotas. . . ."[23] In-country training conducted in the Vietnamese language was the only practical solution to this dilemma.[24]

Every VNAF training requirement was evaluated in late 1969 to see if the training could be conducted in South Vietnam. As a result of that evaluation,

17 hard-core aircraft maintenance courses were identified. These were new courses specially designed to meet VNAF needs. Instead of general helicopter maintenance, for example, a course was designed to teach UH-1 helicopter maintenance since the VNAF would not possess the variety of helicopters usually studied in USAF Air Training Command helicopter courses. The creation of these basic courses marked the beginning of a major transformation in the entire VNAF training program[25/] and forged a closer relationship between the immediate objective of expansion and the long-range goal of self-sufficiency.

Pacer Bravo and Pacer Enhance

Pacer Bravo was the name given to the plan to establish the 17 basic aircraft maintenance skill courses in South Vietnam. (See Figure 3.) To provide the instructors for these courses, 243 VNAF maintenance technicians were carefully selected for training in the United States in specially designed maintenance courses for the specific system they would teach later.[26/] After graduation from the maintenance course, the VNAF students attended the USAF Air Training Command instructor course. Finally, they returned to South Vietnam to establish schools at the VNAF Air Training Center at Nha Trang AB, and satellite schools at Tan Son Nhut AB and Bien Hoa AB.[27/]

USAF assistance did not stop after the instructors were trained. When the VNAF instructors returned to Vietnam, USAF instructors were required to provide additional training for them. On 25 January 1970 the first element of two Mobile Training Teams (MTTs) arrived in South Vietnam to assist the VNAF instructors establish the new courses. From then until 7 May 1971,

13

elements of these two MTTs were in South Vietnam, some for only a few months and others for nearly a year.[28/] Many of the MTT members had taught the new VNAF instructors in the United States, so there was real continuity between preparation and application. (See Figure 4.)

In addition to training VNAF instructors and providing MTTs, the USAF built training aids for the new courses. In all, 869 training aids were specifically designed and fabricated for VNAF use. (See Figures 5 and 6.) These training aids and equipment were assembled at Hill AFB, Utah, where this part of the program was managed.[29/] Then to assure their rapid and safe arrival at the proper destination, a courier accompanied each shipment of training aids from Hill AFB to South Vietnam.[30/]

The Pacer Bravo courses began in March 1970 and by 30 June 1971, there were 5,547 VNAF graduates and an additional 1,332 students were in training.[31/] Pacer Bravo was geared to the immediate requirements of Program II-A and CRIMP, and in fact, but for these requirements, it might not have been attempted.

Pacer Enhance was a related program established to provide expendable items required to support Pacer Bravo. Such items as paper, pencils, and slide projectors were sent to assure that minor as well as major training materials would be available.[32/]

PACER BRAVO COURSES

AFSC	Course Title
301X0	Aircraft Radio Repairman
301X1	Navigation Aid Repairman
421X1	Aircraft Propeller Repairman
421X2	Pneudraulics Repairman
421X3	Aerospace Ground Equipment Repairman
422X0	Instrument Repairman
422X1	Mechanical Accessory Repairman
422X2	Egress Systems Repairman
423X0	Aircraft Electrician
424X0	Fuel System Repairman
431X0	Helicopter Maintenance Repairman
431X1A	Aircraft Maintenance Repairman (Recip)
431X1C	Aircraft Maintenance Repairman (Jet)
432X0	Jet Engine Repairman
432X1	Reciprocating Engine Repairman
461X0	Munitions Specialist
462X0	Weapons Specialist

FIGURE 3

Pacer Bravo: A member of a USAF Mobile Training Team watches a former student conduct instruction on aircraft landing gear systems at Nha Trang AB, South Vietnam.

FIGURE 4

Pacer Bravo Training Aid: Aircraft Engine

FIGURE 5

Pacer Bravo Training Aid: Aircraft Hydraulic System Mockup

FIGURE 6

Although AFLC and the Air Training Command developed a comprehensive plan for the Pacer programs, the AFGP does not have one.[33/] From the evidence that is now available, however, it is clear that expediency often dominated plans. For example, the funds for Pacer Enhance came from at least six different sources. Nonetheless, by July 1971 it was apparent that the Pacer programs represented one of the most successful training experiments ever attempted as part of a United States MAP.[34/]

One problem had not been fully solved by June 1971 and warranted attention. An initial advantage of Pacer Bravo was that the Vietnamese students need not understand English since the in-country courses were taught in Vietnamese. However, most of the technical manuals used by the VNAF were in English. To be more useful to many of the Pacer Bravo graduates, these manuals would have to be translated into Vietnamese although the in-country language training program provided thousands of VNAF personnel with a 50 English Comprehensive Level test score which was considered the minimum required to use a TO.[35/]

The Job Performance Aid (JPA) represented one important effort to overcome this difficulty. JPAs were maintenance manuals written in both Vietnamese and English and designed jointly by the Air Force Systems Command, the Air Force Logistics Command, and the XYZYX Corporation.[36/] Manuals for UH-1, CH-47, and C-123 aircraft had been produced by June 1971. (See Figure 7.) These manuals relied on less language, simpler language, more pictures, and learning by doing, but they were not designed to replace technical manuals needed for guidance in performing the more complicated maintenance tasks. For this, other solutions would have to be found.

Mobile Training Teams

The Pacer Bravo courses established a substantial VNAF training capability in South Vietnam. With this basic experience and with the proven success of the Pacer Bravo courses as encouragement, increased emphasis was placed on employing MTTs in South Vietnam. In late 1969 there were only two MTTs in South Vietnam, but by January 1971 there were seven teams teaching 37 specialized skills.[37/] Between 10 April 1965 and 1 January 1970 only 17 MTTs arrived in South Vietnam. In the next 18 months, 22 teams arrived and three more were scheduled to arrive before the end of 1971. (See Appendix II.)

The MTTs covered a wide variety of specialities including such skills as UNIVAC 1050-II computer operations and counterintelligence. Like the Pacer Bravo courses, the MTT courses made a significant contribution toward increasing VNAF skills and developing training self-sufficiency.

Air Training Center

In January 1970 there were eight schools at the VNAF Air Training Center at Nha Trang AB: a liaison pilot training school, an air liaison officer and forward air controller air ground operations school (ALO/FAC-AGOS), a technical school, a general services school, a communications and electronics school, a military training school, an English language school, and an air base defense school. Together these schools were scheduled to train 4,351 students in Calendar Year (CY) 1970.[38/] The Air Training Center actually exceeded that schedule and trained 6,800 students in CY 1970.[39/]

INSTALL ANTI-COLLISION LIGHT

Install Anti-Collision Light Lamp Bulb.

NOTE

If light is to be installed, go to next page.

1. Check that lens (3) is not cracked or broken. Check that base (6) is not cracked or broken.

2. Place bulb (4) into bulb receptacle (5). Depress and turn bulb to secure.

3. Install lens (3) on base. Place retaining ring (1) at installed position. Tighten screw (2).

CAUTION

Follow-on maintenance action required: Operational Check Anti-Collision Light.

GẮN ĐÈN NGỪA ĐỤNG

Gắn bóng đèn đèn ngừa đụng.

GHI CHÚ

Nếu phải gắn đèn, xem trang kế tiếp.

1. Kiểm kính đèn (3) không bị nứt hoặc bể. Kiểm lê (6) không bị nứt hoặc gãy.

2. Gắn bóng (4) vào đuôi, (5). Ấn và xoay bóng để gắn chắc.

3. Gắn đèn (3) vào đế. Đặt vòng giữ (1) tại vị trí gắn. Siết vít (2).

LƯU Ý

Công tác bảo trì cần được tiếp tục: Phải kiểm hoạt động của đèn ngừa đụng.

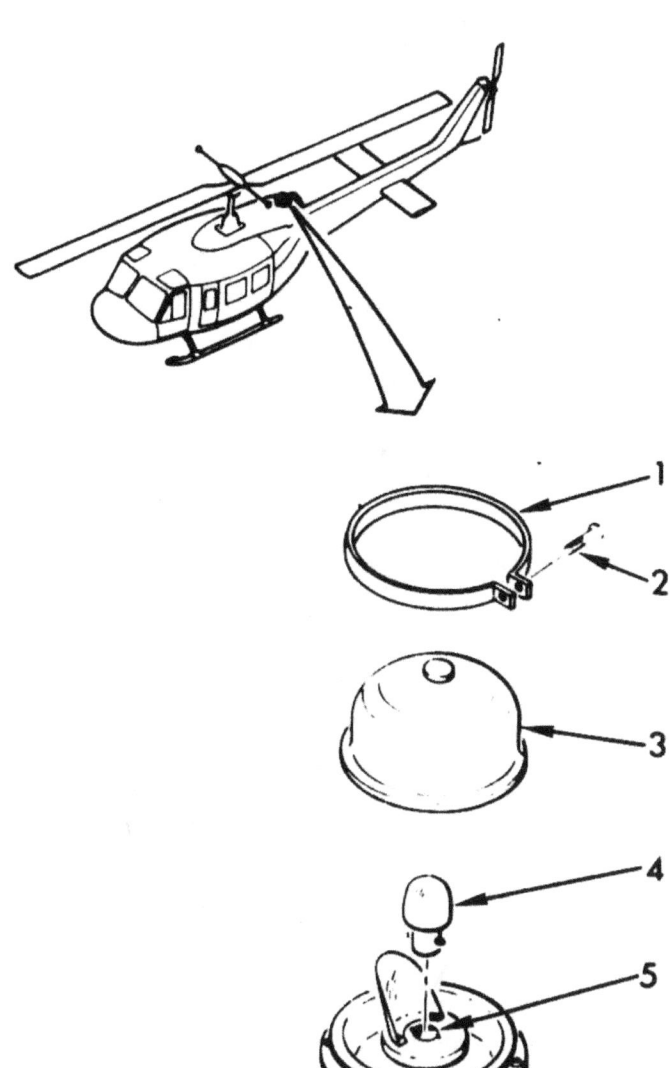

UH-1 Job Performance Aid

Figure 7

Colonel Oanh, Commander of the VNAF Air Training Center at Nha Trang AB prepares for a flight in the first aircraft built in South Vietnam, the TP-1.

FIGURE 8

By 30 June 1971 a command and staff school (equivalent to USAF Squadron Officer School) had been added and the technical school had been expanded considerably. During CY 1971, 12,162 students were programmed to graduate from the Air Training Center schools.[40/] Plans were also under consideration to establish T-41 and T-37 undergraduate pilot training (UPT) as well as helicopter pilot training (HPT) at Nha Trang AB. Navigators were already being trained by the VNAF at Tan Son Nhut AB by June 1971.

The last VNAF helicopter student pilots programmed to be trained in the United States departed South Vietnam on 25 June 1971. By October 1971 there remained only 120 fixed-wing students to enter pilot training in the United States.[41/] The United States had agreed to train 3,334 pilots for the VNAF and as that figure was approached in 1972 the need for a VNAF UPT school would increase. Pilot attrition was expected to be about 7 percent annually. In July 1971 the AFGP Director of Training saw the need to provide the VNAF with the capability to replace attrition losses as the greatest challenge to self-sufficiency yet to be met. The planned UPT course, if adopted, would solve this problem.[42/] Except for pilot training and a few highly technical skills the VNAF was self-sufficient in training by June 1971.[43/]

One development that indicated the technical growth of the VNAF in 1971 was the flight of the TP-1, the first aircraft ever built in South Vietnam. (See Figure 8.) Components of this aircraft shown ready for flight at the Air Training Center, were manufactured by hand at various bases. The engine and the landing gear were the only basic components not built in South Vietnam.[44]

Integrated Training

In January 1970 a 7AF plan provided for integration of VNAF personnel into 7AF units and some United States Army helicopter units for training. This unprecedented plan complemented the VNAF training program and the training provided by USAF MTTs by giving newly trained men experience on the job. (See Figure 9.) By 30 June 1971, 3,385 VNAF personnel had completed this training.[45]

The integrated training program (ITP) required close coordination between the Advisory Group, 7AF, and the VNAF. It was most easily conducted at joint-use bases because there only training was required. At sole-use bases (Cam Ranh Bay, Phu Cat, and Phan Rang) billeting support was also required.

Two types of integrated training were conducted: familiarization, and upgrade. In familiarization training VNAF personnel gained experience but were not awarded a higher skill level. Those successfully completing upgrade training in a 7AF unit, on the other hand, were awarded a higher skill level by the VNAF. Testing by 7AF units was largely subjective. If the Vietnamese trainee performed satisfactorily on the job, he was recommended for upgrade.[46]

Integrated Training: VNAF Airmen work side-by-side with United States Army personnel of the 205th Aviation Company.

FIGURE 9

VNAF On-The-Job Training

VNAF On-the-Job Training (OJT) effectiveness was initially limited by the small number of experienced supervisors available relative to the mass of people to be trained. It was during this period that ITP carried the brunt of the responsibility for providing practical experience to recent technical school graduates.

In January 1970 more VNAF students were trained in ITP than OJT, but by May 1971 the number of students in OJT exceeded the number in ITP. Between January 1970 and June 1971, 4,326 VNAF personnel completed either familiarization or upgrade training through OJT, and 1,934 of these were upgraded.[47]

VNAF personnel were sometimes reluctant to enter upgrade training because when they acquired a higher skill level they also acquired an increased service commitment of several years. During 1970 and early 1971 VNAF personnel were allowed to enter OJT and ITP for either familiarization or upgrade because the results were the same--the man gained increased proficiency in a skill. Improved skills without improved skill levels, however, made personnel planning very difficult. It was almost impossible for USAF managers to measure training progress. This was less of a problem for VNAF managers who relied more on personal contact and less on statistics for personnel management. By March 1971, however, the continued emphasis by USAF advisors on the need for higher skill levels caused a marked shift from familiarization training to upgrade training.[48]

Observations

By June 1971 it was apparent that the most critical facet of establishing VNAF self-sufficiency--a sound and viable training program--was achieved. The break-through had occurred in late 1969 with the Pacer Bravo and Pacer Enhance programs. Throughout 1970 and 1971, MTTs, ITP, VNAF OJT and the Air Training Center steadily improved the competence of VNAF personnel in a wide variety of skills and equipped the VNAF to maintain that competence. Each of these programs played a significant role in the overall accomplishment. Except for pilot training and a few highly technical skills, VNAF self-sufficiency in training appeared assured by mid-1971.

But perhaps the most significant result of the USAF experience in training the VNAF was yet to appear. The emphasis in all previous MAP training programs had been to train foreign students in the United States. The Vietnamese experience should prove that, in the long run, the most productive approach was to train foreign instructors in the United States whenever practical, and then assist them in establishing a training capability in their own country and in their own language. In training the VNAF, the USAF learned the value of exporting the training rather than importing the students.

CHAPTER IV

OPERATIONS

In the Air Force Advisory Group's efforts to improve and modernize the VNAF, air operations received early and sustained emphasis. Because of that emphasis and the VNAF's enthusiastic reponse, VNAF aircrewmen became very adept at tactical air operations. Most USAF observers agreed that the average VNAF pilot was highly qualified by mid-1971, and especially proficient at putting ordnance on target.

A USAF officer with 19 years of service said, "The Vietnamese pilots cannot be surpassed. Time and time again I've watched them drop precisely where the FAC (Forward Air Controllers) directed. And in this kind of war, where allied and enemy troops are often separated by only a few yards, absolute precision is required." [49]

A former head of the Advisory Group, Brigadier General Kendall S. Young, ranked the VNAF in early 1971 as a very effective combat force. The reason was experience. Some VNAF pilots had been flying combat continuously for more than a decade. The average American pilot, on the other hand, had served only one year in Vietnam. [50]

The weaknesses in VNAF operations noted in previous CHECO reports--night and bad-weather flying, helicopter operations, flying hour management, safety consciousness, and air liaison--had been partially eliminated by mid-1971. Every month showed the VNAF taking over a larger share of the air war. During the first quarter of 1971 while devoting 38 percent of its strike effort to Cambodian operations, the VNAF provided 45 percent of all strike sorties flown in South Vietnam. These percentages rose not only because of increasing VNAF activity, but also because of decreasing USAF activity.[51/]

Cambodia

The VNAF flew over 40 percent of the total USAF and VNAF attack sorties supporting Cambodian ground operations in 1970-1971.[52/] The early activation of a medium-lift helicopter squadron gave the VNAF a capability for lift support into Cambodia as well as close air support, although providing a capability for cross-border operations was not explicitly a feature of the I&M Program. Most significantly, the planning for VNAF support of battalion-size ARVN forces deployed in Cambodia was done almost wholly by the VNAF itself. The planning included interdiction, close air support of the ARVN, and troop lift.[53/]

During the initial phase of the Cambodian operation (May and June 1970) when both United States and South Vietnamese troops were committed, the VNAF flew 2,897 attack sorties compared to the USAF's 8,579. When only ARVN troops were left in Cambodia, the VNAF's proportion of sorties rose.[54/]

At times VNAF effectiveness drew mixed reactions. The F-5, A-1, and A-37 pilots were complimented for their spirit and performance by USAF and press observers and criticized in the press for a lack of restraint while bombing a land which had for centuries been a traditional enemy of

VNAF A-1 on a Bombing Mission

FIGURE 10

Vietnam.[55]

In December 1970 the VNAF rated high marks for operation "Eagle Jump" which was mounted to relieve enemy pressure around the provincial center of Kampong Cham, and to open Highway 7 which connected it with Saigon. With only short notice the VNAF planned and executed its part of the operation: the movement of troops and supplies from Tan Son Nhut AB and Thien Ngon AB to Kampong Cham airfield and resupply for the two week operation. Relying primarily on the C-47s and C-119s of Tan Son Nhut's 33d Wing, and to a lessor extent on helicopters from MR 3 and 4, thirty-two hundred troops and two million pounds of cargo were moved. The USAF Advisory Group reported that "Aircraft take-off and arrival times were met with precision, and changes were taken in stride. They did a truly professional job."[56] The operation gave the VNAF a tremendous boost in individual and unit espirit and enhanced the confidence of those observing the Vietnamization program.

In a significant reverse on 22 January 1971, however, the VNAF lost 15 aircraft on a single night when Communist mortar fire hit the airfield at Phnom Penh, Cambodia. Nine UH-1s, three O-1s, one U-17, and two AC-47s were destroyed.[57]

Figures available for the first six months of 1971 show that 27 percent of VNAF aircraft battle damage occurred in Cambodia. The total number of aircraft damaged in battle during this period was 301. In May alone 70 aircraft were hit, 27 of them in Cambodia.[58] The Cambodian campaigns showed, among other things, that the VNAF had the capacity to surge to an increased number of sorties when necessary. But that surge in Cambodia delayed some training programs and tempered the pace of operations in both South Vietnam and Laos.

Laos

Air support for the ARVN incursion into Laos in February and March of 1971, Lam Son 719, came primarily from the USAF. This operation revealed the differing points of view held by 7AF which planned the air support, and the USAF advisors who were concerned with VNAF I&M. The 7AF planners had one thing in mind--the success of the operation--and they were reluctant to rely on the VNAF. The USAF advisors saw the need for the VNAF to get experience in operations like Lam Son 719 which they might have to carry out alone in the future. Although VNAF helicopters and forward air observers were used from the start, VNAF A-37s were not allowed to take part in the operation until a month after it had started.[59/]

When they were employed during the latter half of the operation, VNAF A-37s from Da Nang flew over 1,000 sorties on both sides of the border. None were lost, but one aircraft was hit.[60/]

Throughout the operation an average of 16 VNAF UH-1s and H-34s operated from a forward base at Dong Ha, South Vietnam, and flew over 5,500 sorties transporting troops and supplies into fire bases in Laos. On the return flights they evacuated the dead and wounded.[61/]

During Lam Son 719 some VNAF helicopter pilots were criticized for poor navigation.[62/] When five well-known journalists and Lieutenant General Do Cao Tri, the ARVN Commander in Cambodia, were killed in two separate helicopter crashes the losses were widely attributed to navigational error. This gave a distorted view of the capability of VNAF helicopter pilots. Some of the difficulty encountered during the Lam Son operation might well have been the result of the recent expansion and reorganization of the 1st AD and the consequent limited experience of some helicopter crewmen.[63/]

Forty-five English speaking VNAF forward air observers flew in the back seat of USAF OV-10s during the operation. The VNAF observers helped direct approximately 2,000 strike sorties by translating between the ground commanders and the USAF FAC who flew the plane and directed USAF fighters. VNAF O-1 FAC aircraft were not used.[64/]

Some difficulty was experienced when teaming VNAF forward air observers (as translators) with USAF FACs. Some USAF FACs said that at times the VNAF observers were late for the missions or did not show up at all, claiming medical or other excuses.[65/] Flights in the OV-10 often made the VNAF observers sick. They had come from VNAF O-1 aircraft and were not accustomed to rocket passes in the comparative high performance of the OV-10. Once airsick, they were generally useless to the FAC for the rest of the mission.[66/]

The inability of some VNAF observers to successfully translate was a more serious problem and one reflected in the FACs daily intelligence summaries.[67/] When the VNAF observer failed him, the FAC was forced to rely on English-speaking Vietnamese personnel with the ground units, and frequently these men held critical positions within their units and could not be easily spared for interpreting. Occasionally the FAC had to work from his own visual assessment of the ground situation, or the unit, for lack of communication, did not get tactical air support. Most of the VNAF observers performed well even though shortcomings were reported from several sources. One USAF FAC was quick to point out that when the VNAF observers spoke English well they were a great asset ". . . since there weren't many English speaking Vietnamese on the ground."[68]

VNAF FACs were not used during the operation due to their O-1's limited capability. The OV-10 had better radio equipment, better performance over the mountainous terrain, and better survivability against enemy anti-aircraft fire.[69] For similar reasons, VNAF A-37s were initially excluded from the Lam Son area. Nor were any VNAF officers in the direct air support center (DASC) to observe the operation. The emphasis was on performance--not training or experience for the VNAF.[70]

One month after the operation began VNAF A-37s were allowed to take part, largely because of Advisory Group efforts.[71] The Group's position was that Vietnamization had the highest priority in Vietnam, that the Laos operation had been mounted to protect the Vietnamization process, and that the VNAF pilots could use the experience supporting troops in an environment like Laos. Seventh Air Force officials considered the A-37 not to have enough range and loiter capability.[72] Furthermore, since the VNAF had the primary support role for the ARVN in Cambodia, some thought VNAF resources too limited to permit operations in Laos also. The demonstrated ability of the VNAF to provide effective support in both areas allayed this concern and again confirmed that the VNAF had a surge capability.

The A-37's performance in Lam Son 719 tended to dispel its reputation for poor survivability in an intense antiaircraft environment. As one American FAC who had taken part in the operation said, "We really admired the VNAF A-37 pilots' accuracy and their guts in going down low. Any time we asked them to make two passes--a dry run first--low and slow, they did it. As a result, no one was hitting targets any better than they were. It was very, very thrifty when they were delivering."[73/]

The role of the VNAF in furnishing tactical air support was nevertheless small compared with the USAF contribution. Of the 1,004 VNAF A-37 sorties flown during Lam Son 719, only 436 were flown in the Laos battle area.[74/] The U.S. forces flew 8,512 tactical strike sorties.

Conclusion

USAF improvement and modernization efforts contributed substantionally to the Vietnamization of the air war in 1970 and 1971. Improved equipment, increased strength, and declining enemy activity allowed the VNAF to gradually assume a larger responsibility for the air war as USAF combat units were withdrawn. From January 1969 to the early months of 1971, the VNAF role in air operations quadrupled. (See Figure 11.)

CHAPTER V

TACTICAL AIR CONTROL SYSTEM

The VNAF Tactical Air Control System (TACS) was improved significantly in 1970 and 1971. In January 1970 the Tactical Air Control Center (TACC) and the Direct Air Support Centers (DASCs) were operated jointly by the USAF and the VNAF. By July 1971 the VNAF had assumed control of the TACC as well as control of the DASCs in MR 2, MR 3, and MR 4. The DASC in MR 1 was under joint control, but scheduled for transfer to the VNAF in August 1971.[75]

Air Operations Command

The VNAF Air Operations Command (AOC) had operational responsibility for all VNAF air assets. Operational control, mission planning, and execution were ". . . vested entirely in the AOC."[76] This organization did not correspond to the command and control structure in the USAF where the Deputy Chief of Staff for Operations exercised operational control. Operational control was a command function in the VNAF rather than a staff function as in the USAF.

The AOC exercised control through the TACC ordinarily, but it was prepared to exercise more direct control. An advanced AOC party composed of personnel from both the AOC headquarters and the TACC could be deployed when conditions warranted.[77]

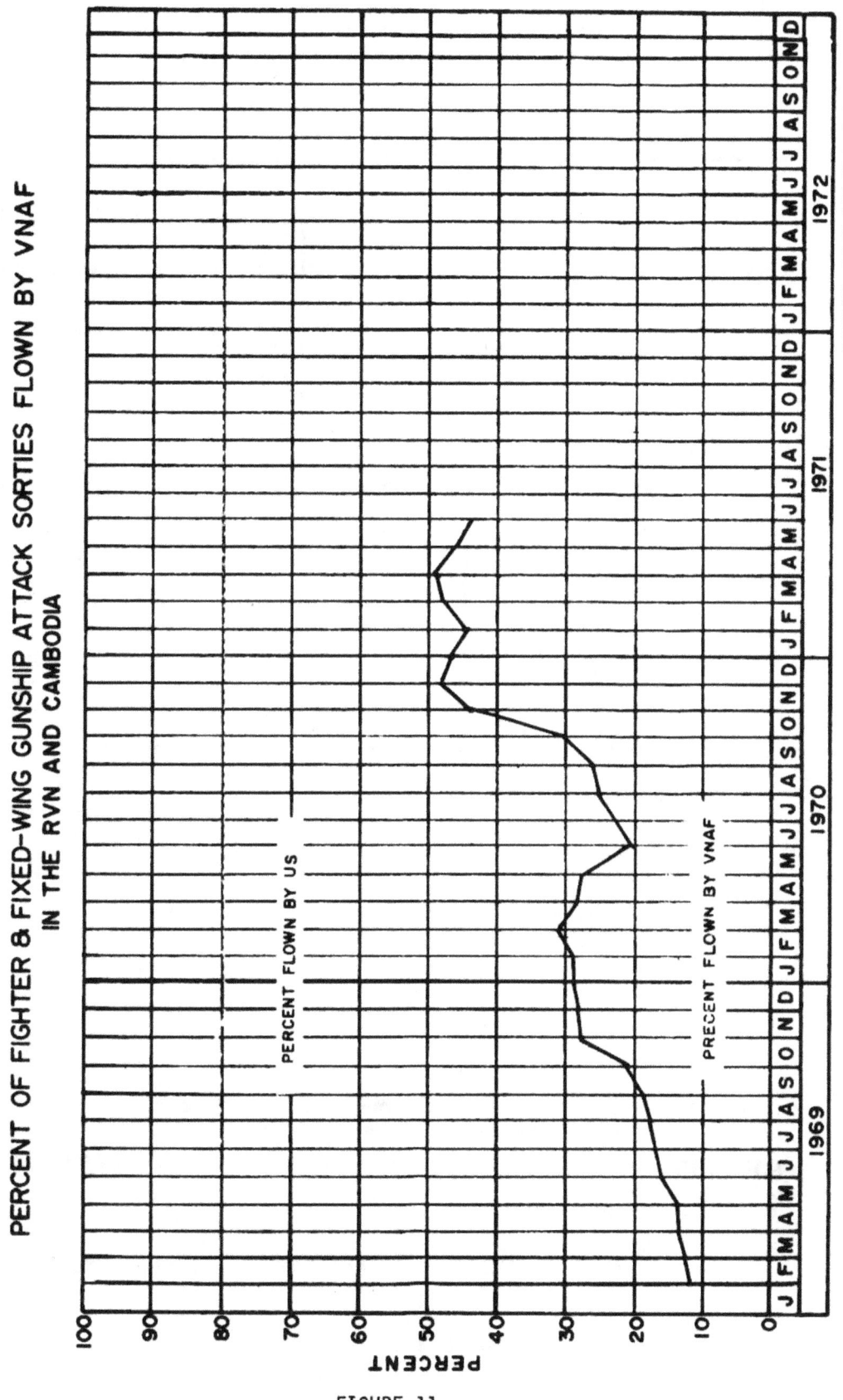

FIGURE 11

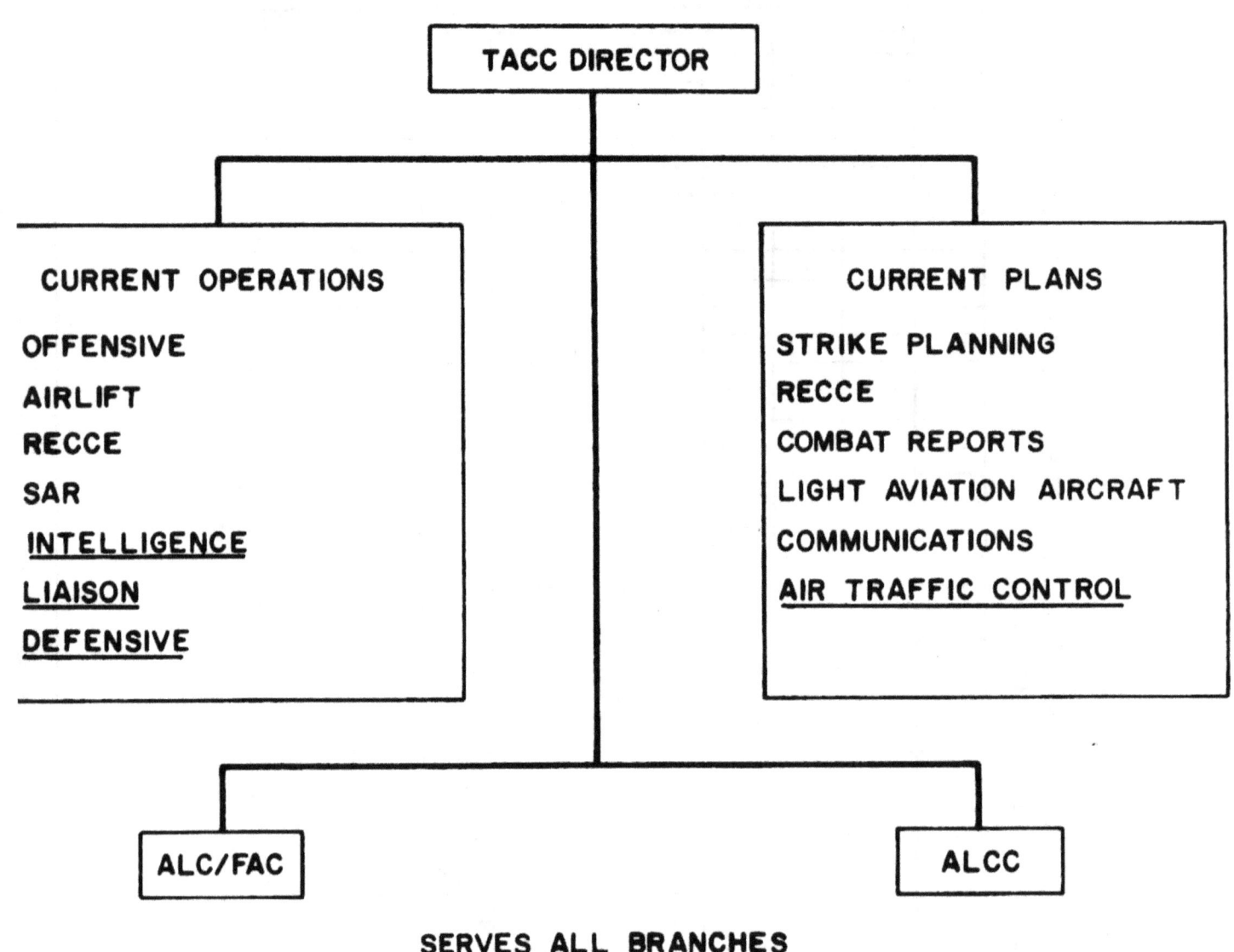

VNAF TACTICAL AIR CONTROL CENTER

SOURCE: BRIEFING, "VNAF COMMAND AND CONTROL SYSTEM SELF-SUFFICIENCY"
BY LT COL J.H. MATHEWS, 7AF-DOCP.

FIGURE 12

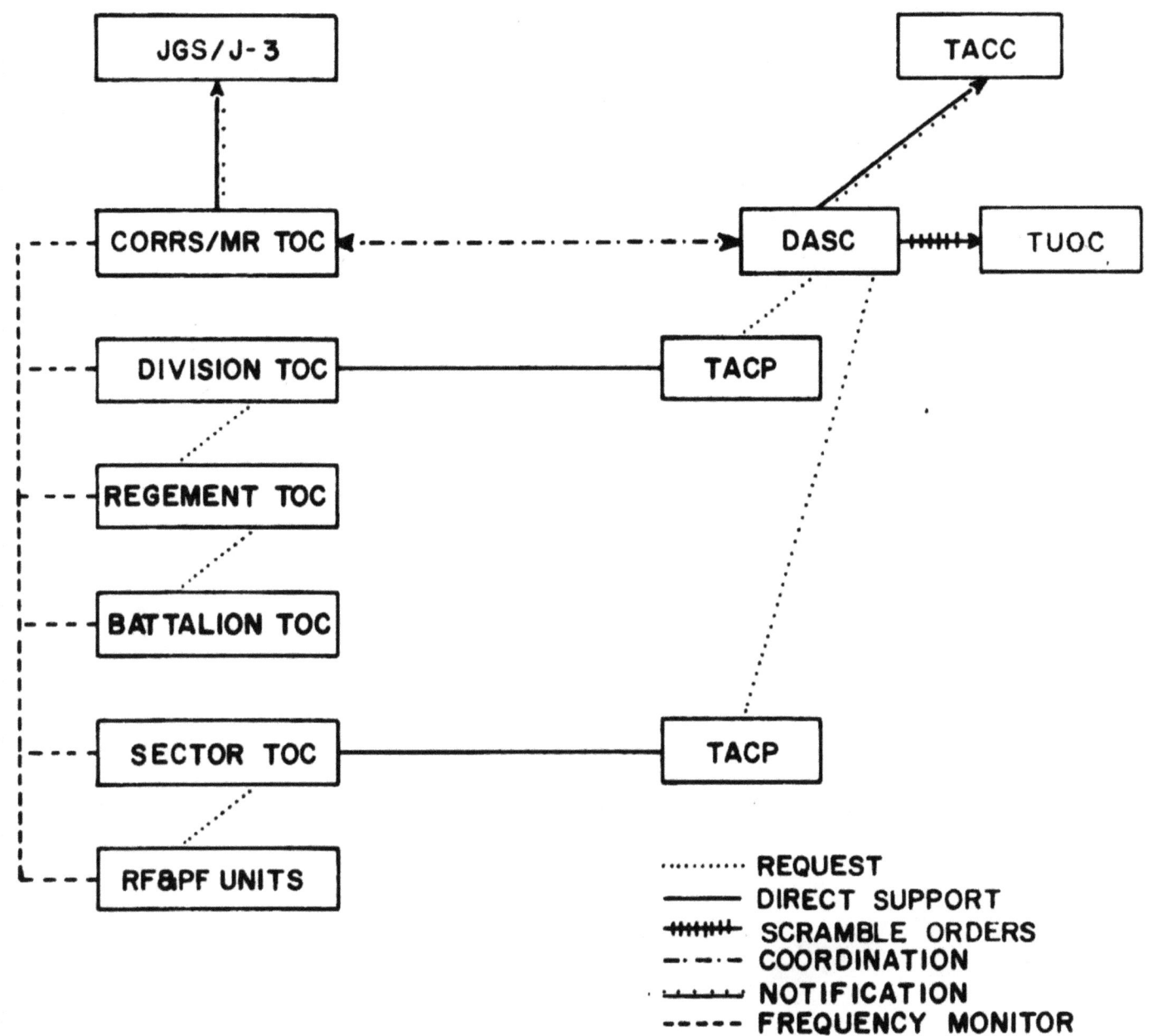

TACTICAL AIR SUPPORT IMMEDIATE NET.

SOURCE: BRIEFING, "VNAF COMMAND AND CONTROL SYSTEM SELF-SUFFICIENCY,"

BY LT COL J.H. MATHEWS, 7AF-DOCP

FIGURE 13

The advanced AOC party, deployed in 1970 and 1971 at Kampong Cham airport, Cambodia, exercised the delegated authority of the AOC during ". . . the Eagle operations." This was a series of operations intended to regain control of Cambodian Route 7. The commander of the advanced AOC party exercised control over all airlift, strike, and helicopter sorties employed in the geographic area of operations.[78/] Sorties were allocated by the VNAF TACC and when they entered Cambodia they came under the operational control of the advanced AOC party.

The VNAF and the USAF shared the TACC for South Vietnam until June 1971 when joint control of the TACC was terminated. After that date VNAF air assets were controlled by the VNAF TACC and USAF air assets were controlled by the 7AF TACC. After June 1971 the VNAF TACC reported to the AOC. The commander of the AOC was also the director of the VNAF TACC. There were no USAF advisors assigned to the VNAF TACC or AOC "in view of the highly independent nature of the AOC commander incumbent and the anticipated difficulty of getting an AFGP advisor/counterpart established and accepted. . . ."[79/] Instead, assistance was provided at lower levels of command.

One area of recognized weakness in the VNAF TACS was the Air Liaison Officer function and this was one point where lower level assistance could be provided. The VNAF requested Lt. Col. Marland O. Marshall be assigned as an advisor to the Senior VNAF ALO on the AOC staff. Lt. Col. Marshall enjoyed the respect and esteem of the VNAF earned during three tours in the Republic of Vietnam. The AOC further requested that Lt. Col. Marshall be returned to Vietnam in MAAG duty ". . . so that his knowledge and experience could continue to be of benefit to the VNAF."[80/] It is apparent therefore, that while the AOC commander did not have a counterpart assigned, he did have an advisor.

Tactical Air Control Center

The VNAF TACC was responsible for control of air assets as directed by the AOC. The TACC had four major organizational divisions: Current Operations, Current Plans, an Airlift Control Center, and an Air Liaison Officer and Forward Air Controller section. (See Figure 12.)

Although responsible for operational control, the TACC customarily delegated that responsibility to the DASCs unless aircraft from several Air Divisions were to be employed simultaneously.[81/] In that event, the TACC exercised control. The TACC also exercised divert authority on all preplanned VNAF sorties to support emergency or immediate requests.[82/] More often, however, the authority for operational control was delegated to the DASCs which operated with considerable independence in their respective Military Regions (MR).

Direct Air Support Centers

By August 1971 all the DASCs were to be controlled by the VNAF. VNAF personnel had worked in the DASCs for several years alongside their American counterparts. Each had controlled his own country's air resources

and they coordinated when necessary. Once the USAF departed the VNAF
DASCs would be self-sufficient.[83/]

The DASCs were collocated with the Corps Tactical Operations Centers
(TOCs) in each MR. VNAF targets were ". . . usually generated by the
Military Region Commander through the DASC. . . ." VNAF targeting was
thus dominated by the ARVN.[84/] The DASC's fragged sorties provided
details (including ARVN established priorities) of preplanned missions
to the TACC, and monitored the immediate request net.[85/]

The relationship between the various elements and users of the TACS
was often confusing. One senior USAF officer described it as ". . . a
nightmare to the American mind."[86/] Within a MR the VNAF flew missions
against targets selected by the ARVN commander, approved by the province
chief, and fragged by the DASC. If more tactical air support was needed
in one MR than could be provided by the assigned AD, sortie requests were
sent through the DASCs and the TACC to the RVNAF Joint General Staff (JGS)
which, if it approved the request, directed another AD to provide the needed
sorties. These were then fragged and controlled by the TACC.

Immediate Request Net

Requests for immediate or emergency air support from Tactical Air
Control Parties (TACPs) were relayed to the DASCs through the Corps
Tactical Operations Center (TOC). The DASC then diverted or scrambled
aircraft required for support. (See Figure 13.) The VNAF did not keep

a dedicated stand-by force available for immediate support but preplanned sorties were on alert for two hours before scheduled take-off and these were available if needed. Immediate airlift and helicopter support was handled the same way. Divert requests were monitored at each intermediate level; five minutes after a request, it was considered approved if higher headquarters did not intervene, and the DASC diverted or scrambled the necessary aircraft.[87/]

Air Liaison Officers and Forward Air Controllers

The Senior Air Liaison Officer (ALO) at the TACC had operational control of the TACPs. Each TACP was composed of an ALO, radio operators, and administrative personnel. (See Figure 14.) Until June 1971 the DASCs exercised operational control of the TACPs, but, allegedly because ". . . DASC Directors were misusing the ALO. . . ." operational control was transferred to the TACC. FACs were under the operational control of the ALO.[88/]

The weakest area in the VNAF TACS in 1970 was the ALO and FAC function. The ALOs were occasionally pilot training wash-outs, and this undermined the prestige of most ALOs. Some ALOs were therefore unable to effectively advise the senior army officers to whom they were detailed. To correct this, experienced field grade VNAF officers were being assigned as ALOs for a one to two-year tour.[89/]

VNAF FACs were being trained to direct USAF air strikes. By July 1971, there were 29 pilots and 57 observers qualified, and it was anticipated that with the addition of the 27 FACs then undergoing training, the VNAF

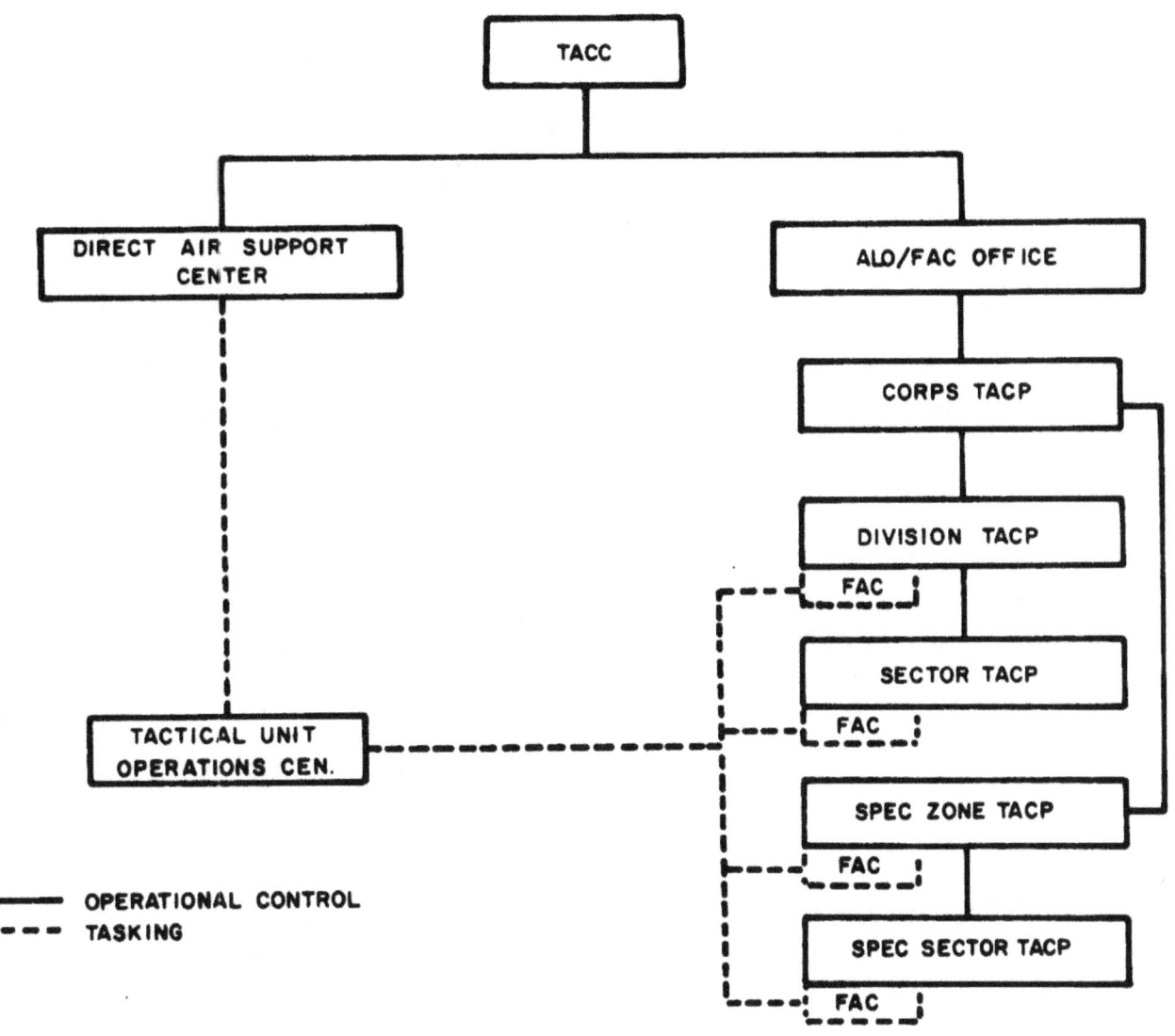

TACTICAL AIR SUPPORT OPERATIONS.

SOURCE: BRIEFING, "VNAF COMMAND AND CONTROL SYSTEM SELF-SUFFICIENCY," BY LT COL J. H. MATHEWS, 7th AF-DOCP.

FIGURE 14

VNAF O-1 Forward Air Controller Marking a Target

FIGURE 15

would have the capability to control all USAF and VNAF air strikes in South Vietnam.[90/]

Equipment difficulties plagued the FACs during most of this period. Their O-1 aircraft were not equipped with adequate panel lighting for night operations or with reliable radio aids. The necessary modifications were funded in mid-1971 and the appropriate kits were expected to arrive in September 1971.[91/]

Airlift Control Center

The Airlift Control Center (ALCC) in TACC was responsible for processing all preplanned airlift requests. These requests came from three sources: the President of the Republic of Vietnam, the VNAF transportation division, and the Central Logistics Command of the RVNAF Joint General Staff (JGS). (See Figure 16.)

The ALCC matched resources with the airlift requests when possible. If the requests exceeded the resources, the requests were returned to the originators to resolve priorities.[92/] For example, if the JGS and the VNAF transportation division submitted competing requests the ALCC did not resolve the conflict. It was unclear how conflicting requests were resolved, but requests made by the President probably took precedence, and those made by the JGS probably received second consideration. Once resource allocation was decided, the ALCC prepared a daily airlift frag and disseminated it to the DASCs.[93/]

Air Control and Warning

In addition to the DASCs, the TACC had operational control of VNAF Air Control and Warning (AC&W) operations. In July 1971 this capability was not developed, but training had been initiated for both air intercept operators and flight crews. Air intercept operator training was being conducted by the 505th Tactical Control Group (USAF) at Tan Son Nhut Air Base. When fuel permitted, practice intercepts were conducted using VNAF fighters returning from strike missions. [94/]

Although under the operational control of the TACC, the elements of the AC&W organization were assigned to the VNAF AC&W Group at Tan Son Nhut. These elements were operationally ready in July 1971 except for the absence of qualified air intercept operators and technicians. The operators were expected to be trained and qualified by late 1971. Self-sufficiency was expected to be accomplished by December 1971 with the exception of communications and electronics (C&E) maintenance. The VNAF had requested 24 radar maintenance technicians and nine ground power and air conditioning specialists be assigned by the USAF to augment the AC&W Group until June 1972. [95/]

In July 1971 a secure Tactical Teletype System, linking the TACC with all TACS elements including Base Communications Center, Tactical Unit Operations Centers (TUOCs), AC&W sites, and the DASCs, was installed in the VNAF TACC. This communications net was expected to be fully operational in early 1973 when all the terminals were installed. [96/]

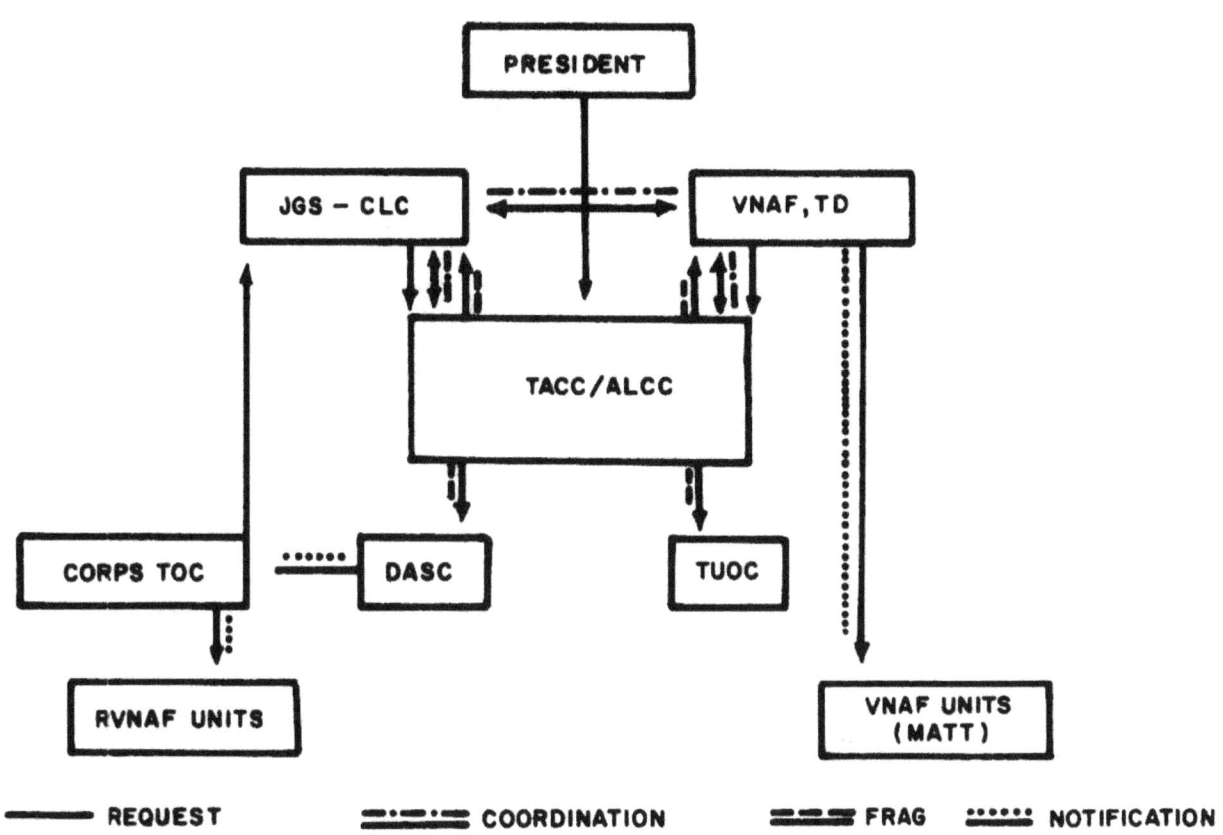

SOURCE: BRIEFING, "VNAF COMMAND AND CONTROL SYSTEM SELF-SUFFICIENCY," BY LT COL J. H. MATHEWS, 7th AF - DOCP.

FIGURE 16

Thus the VNAF TACS was approaching self-sufficiency in mid-1971. In the TACC and the DASCs, the VNAF was assuming responsibility for the tactical air war. Advisory assistance was successfully being devoted to improve Air Defense, FAC, and ALO capability. These areas would improve as training continued and necessary equipment arrived.

CHAPTER VI

HELICOPTERS

Nowhere has the impact of the I&M Program been so readily apparent as on the VNAF helicopter force. Beginning in January 1970 with 112 aircraft and 110 operationally ready crews, the VNAF grew to 413 aircraft and 365 combat ready crews by July 1971. Nor was this the end of the helicopter expansion. CRIMP planning called for the addition of three more UH-1 squadrons and one CH-47 squadron by June 1972 as well as the conversion of the last H-34 squadron to UH-1s. This would give the VNAF 18 helicopter squadrons and 532 aircraft. (See Appendix I.) This force represented almost half the final VNAF force structure of 1,300 aircraft authorized by CRIMP. [97/]

Impressive as this expansion was, it did not enable the VNAF helicopter force to match that of the U.S. Army at its maximum strength in South Vietnam. For example, in 1969 the VNAF flew only one percent of all the helicopter sorties flown in South Vietnam. [98/] By 1971, the increase in VNAF capability and the decline in the number of sorties flown by the U.S. Army changed the statistics and the VNAF share of the sortie total increased from one percent to 12 percent by June 1971. [99/] Nevertheless, the VNAF's limited helicopter resources would require thrifty employment.

Doctrine

The VNAF's growing helicopter capability was never expected to equal that of the U.S. Army. This condition led to a sharp controversy between the ARVN and the VNAF.

The ARVN had become accustomed to the massive helicopter airlift available from the U.S. Army and the decline in helicopter airlift demanded a conservation of resources. When the ARVN commanders received support from the U.S. Army, it was more freely available than from the VNAF. The result was an ARVN assertion that VNAF support was inadequate. [100/]

This conflict stemmed from both declining numbers of helicopters available and from differing management concepts between the U.S. Army and the VNAF. The U.S. Army tended to dedicate helicopters to units: a user oriented system which the ARVN liked. Since the VNAF was to have only one-tenth the total number of helicopters formerly available from the U.S. Army, VNAF resources had to be managed differently. [101/]

The VNAF's countercharges against the ARVN emphasized inefficient use of helicopters. The ARVN claimed the VNAF was not responsive to their needs--that aircraft showed up late or not at all or in smaller numbers than requested. The dispute threatened RVNAF combat effectiveness and action was clearly needed to resolve this conflict.

That action came in February 1971 when the JGS published Directive 310-19 for the management and employment of helicopters. [102/] This directive established ". . . management procedures for helicopters on combat operations, medevac, supply and liaison missions, etc. . . ." and it applied to all of the RVNAF.

Directive 310-19 was a clear and detailed description of how helicopters were to be managed. Not only did it reveal a clear grasp of the problem facing the RVNAF, but it indicated that the JGS had the ability to solve it. In July 1971 it was too early to evaluate the directive's operational effect.

In Directive 310-19, the JGS established procedures for operational,* medevac, supply, liaison, command and control, and airdrop missions. Priorities were also established among these different missions.

Operational missions held highest priority and included the landing or extracting of troops during day or night. Details of landing zone (LZ) preparation, size, and use were described, as well as the constraints on the route of flight and the responsibilities of the troops to be lifted. [103/]

Medevac missions received second priority overall, but various medevac priorities were also established to classify the wounded personnel to be evacuated. Each MR was to have a minimum of two medevac helicopters and crews on fifteen-minute alert, but the Directive also stressed that in an emergency any helicopter could be used. [104/]

*An "operational mission" was one flown to move combat troops into battle. As used in Directive 310-19, VNAF "operational missions" are similar to United States Army helicopter assault missions.

Supply missions received third priority and were to be employed only when surface and fixed-wing supply could not be employed. Liaison missions received fourth priority.[105/]

Directive 310-19 also discussed the operational availability of helicopters and stressed that "daily flying hours must be maintained at a normal level in order to keep aircraft availability at a maximum and stabilize the maintenance and repair plan." The Directive went on to specify the number of flying hours for helicopters and crews, and the schedule for new units to achieve full operational capability.[106/]

Direction 310-19 was thus a comprehensive statement of RVNAF helicopter doctrine. It was aimed at resolving the conflict between the ARVN and the VNAF and it did so on VNAF terms.

Personnel

Directive 310-19 resolved helicopter doctrine, but this was not the only area in which helicopter effectiveness could be improved. By July 1970 most VNAF helicopter squadrons had reached C-2 combat readiness* although many of the crews were newly trained. Experience was shallow and would be diluted further in 1972 as more helicopter squadrons were activated. This same difficulty was encountered in maintenance, and in both areas time was needed to gain experience.

*For a description of the VNAF C-ratings, see the Glossary.

Training of helicopter pilots in the United States was nearing completion in July 1971. The training program for helicopter crews and maintenance personnel had been very successful, particularly the ITP conducted by the Army in conjunction with the transfer of helicopters to the VNAF. 107/

By July 1971 the VNAF helicopter force had nearly quadrupled from 109 authorized in January 1970 to 417 in June 1971. The number of sorties flown had increased fourfold and the VNAF percentage of helicopter missions flown in South Vietnam had increased from 1.24 percent to 12.08 percent. This expansion and growth was the result of training and equipment authorized by CRIMP. It was apparent that the helicopter force, though still faced with some problems, was improved and modernized and that the JGS was attempting to effectively manage it as an integral part of the RVNAF military establishment.

CHAPTER VII

FIGHTERS

The period from January 1970 to July 1971 was one of improved performance and limited expansion for VNAF fighter squadrons. Sixty fighter aircraft were added to the force including six RF-5s. But at the end of this period, the number of combat ready fighter crews had increased by only 7 with an additional 11 formed and not yet combat ready.[108/] Significantly, this was 63 crews less than authorized. (See Appendix IV.)

Performance

The shortage of combat ready crews had a noticeable impact on the combat capability of the fighter force as measured by C Ratings. In January 1970 all the fighter squadrons were rated C-1. By July 1971, only four squadrons retained the C-1 rating. Two squadrons were rated C-2 due to crew shortages; two squadrons were rated C-2 due to maintenance difficulty, and one squadron was rated C-3 because it had only ten combat ready crews of 27 authorized.[109/]

Even with declining C-Ratings the VNAF percentage of attack sorties increased throughout this period. This came about for several reasons: the tempo of the air war in South Vietnam waned, the number of available USAF attack sorties declined, and the VNAF was able to establish a sortie rate consistent with the demands of the combat situation. For example, in 1971 the VNAF sortie rate approximated that of the USAF, both rates declining during the wet season and increasing during the dry season. The VNAF was maturing in flying hour management. This was a big step toward self-sufficiency and it was due to the success of the I&M program. (See Figure 17.)

There was a noticeable decline in ground operations in South Vietnam during 1970 and 1971.[110/] Consequently, there was less need for close air support and thus fewer attack sorties were flown.

Total USAF sortie activity in Southeast Asia was lower in June 1971 than any month since 1966.[111/] This trend in USAF air activity was the result of withdrawal of units and continued emphasis on Vietnamizing the war. In September 1971 USAF disengagement was expected to accelerate, thus causing the VNAF to assume even greater responsibility for the total air effort.[112/]

In 1970 and 1971 the VNAF conducted extensive air operations in Cambodia and by June 1971 23.2 percent of the total attack sorties flown by the VNAF were close air support missions in Cambodia. Additionally, the VNAF flew sorties in Laos in 1971 to support Lam Son 719. In Laos only 256 attack sorties were flown, but in Cambodia the VNAF flew over 1,000 strike sorties per month during the first five months of 1971.[113/]

The growing role of the VNAF in close air support was a convincing indication of VNAF capability--a capability not clearly reflected by the VNAF fighter squadrons' C Rating. It was also proof that CRIMP was effectively improving and modernizing the Vietnamese Air Force.

USAF ATTACK SORTIES AND VNAF STRIKE SORTIES
REPUBLIC OF VIETNAM, 1970-71

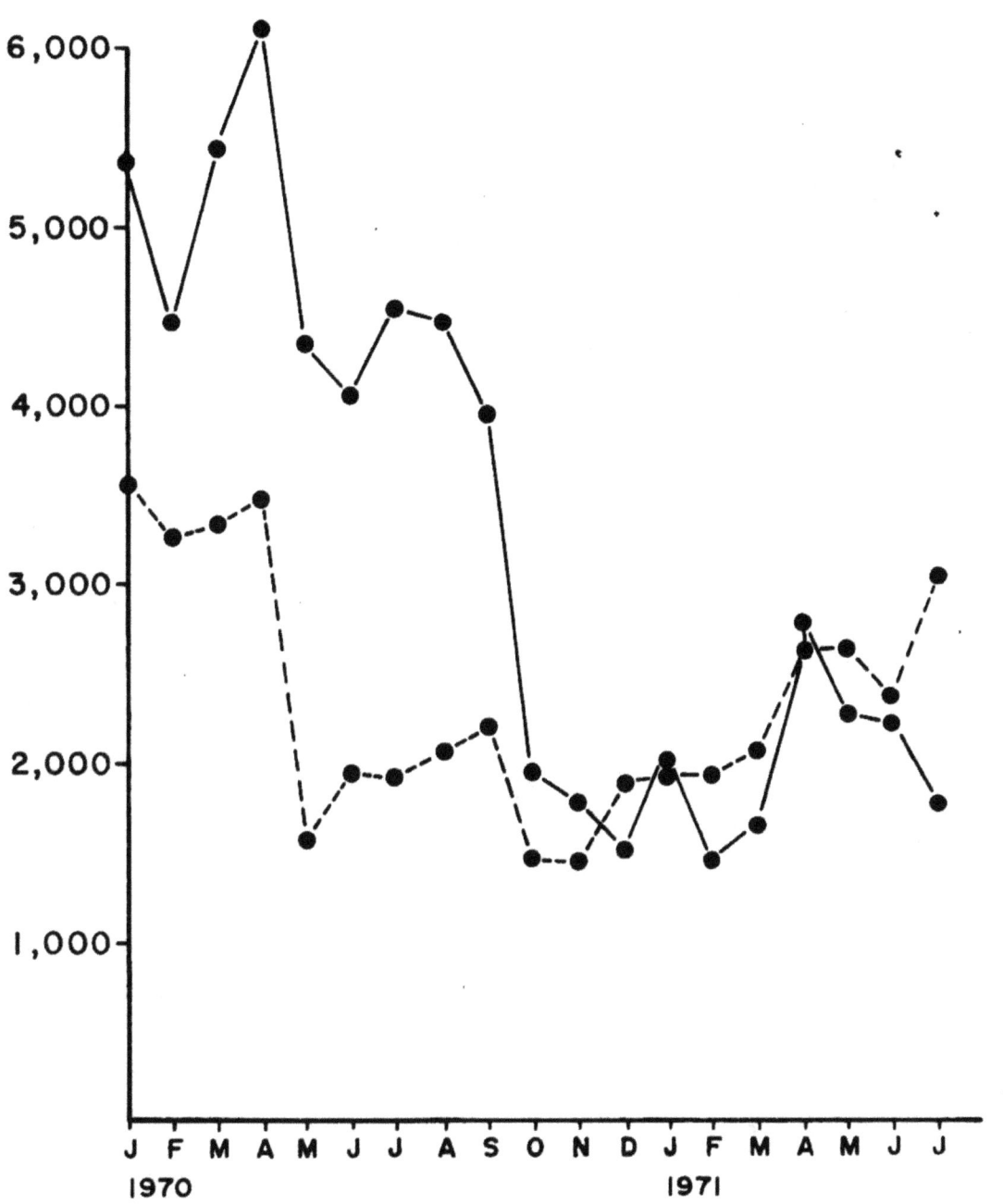

USAF ———
VNAF -----

SOURCE: 7AF COMMAND STATUS BOOK
DEC 1970 AND JUN 1971

FIGURE 17

Limited Expansion

But the C Ratings did indicate weak areas in fighter capability--areas that needed attention. The chief reason for the decline in C Ratings in the fighter squadrons during 1970 and 1971 was a shortage of combat ready crews. This was the result of the increase of aircraft and squadrons without a corresponding increase in the training of new fighter pilots.

In 1970 the highest priority was given to helicopter requirements and 791 helicopter pilots were trained while only 42 pilots were trained in fighters.[114/] In 1971, the emphasis remained on training helicopter pilots. By 1 July 348 helicopter pilots had graduated from training courses in the United States. During the same period 31 fighter pilots received training.[115/]

There was a limit to the pilot training candidates the VNAF could produce and in 1970 and 1971, most candidates entered helicopter training. The shortage of fighter pilots was thus a result of priorities. It was a problem that would be solved as more pilots became available.

A similar shortage occurred in maintenance personnel due to the priority of helicopter squadron activations. Thus, this was a period of limited expansion for the VNAF fighter force--a period when the force became more experienced and gained additional equipment, but failed to gain all the necessary personnel.

Expanded Operational Capability

The operational capability of the VNAF fighter force was expanded during this period in two significant areas--all weather bombing and air defense.

In 1970 the AFGP emphasized the need for the VNAF to improve its night and all-weather capability. Night operations in particular were stressed since that was when the enemy was most active. Therefore, the VNAF began a night-flying training program. [116/]

The program started with a VNAF instrument training course. Fighter pilots assigned to A-37s and A-1s were then introduced to flare techniques to illuminate a target before bombing it. The next step was to train the pilots in "Combat Skyspot" operations--a radar controlled method for delivering ordnance. By mid-1971 all A-37 squadrons were Combat Skyspot qualified and the A-1 squadrons were in training.

Strategic Air Command (SAC) MSQ-77 radar sites were used for training and actual combat drops, but SAC planned to remove the sites from South Vietnam. The AFGP therefore requested a substitute system which could be given to the VNAF. In May 1971 the Beacon Only Bombing System (BOBS) was selected. The first BOBS sets were to be delivered in August 1972, giving the VNAF an all-weather high altitude day-and-night bombing capability. [117/]

VNAF Airmen Loading Bombs on an A-37

FIGURE 18

VNAF F-5 Fighters

FIGURE 19

The VNAF also trained for air defense in preparation for the withdrawal of USAF air defense forces from South Vietnam and the activation of a CRIMP authorized F-5E intercepter squadron. The 522nd squadron at Bien Hoa AB, already equipped with F-5 fighters, began training in 1971 using AIM-9B Sidewinder missiles and 20 millimeter (mm) cannon. After training, the F-5 squadron would assume responsibility for air defense during visual meteorological conditions (VMC).[118/] The VNAF would not have an all-weather air defense capability, even when the F-5E squadron was activated, and activation was not programmed until fiscal year (FY) 1974.

There was cause for concern about the VNAF air defense capability in 1971. One 7AF study indicated that North Vietnam could attack Saigon with eight IL-28s and could attack MR 1 with about 100 MIG-21s, 34 MIG-19s, and 136 MIG-15s and MIG-17s.[119/]

In February 1971 serious consideration was given to adding as many as four more F-5E squadrons to the CRIMP authorization, but by May the addition of only two squadrons seemed more probable. This force would be complemented by two ARVN air defense battalions armed with 32 twin 40mm guns and 48 quadruple 50mm guns.[120/]

Thus the VNAF fighter force in July 1971 was a much more capable force than at the beginning of CRIMP. Air defense, all weather bombing, and out-of-country operations added new dimensions to VNAF capabilities and self-sufficiency--and that was the goal of CRIMP during this period.

CHAPTER VIII

GUNSHIPS

In January 1970 the VNAF had one AC-47 gunship squadron with 18 assigned aircraft. This squadron flew 62.2 percent of all fixed-wing gunship missions flown in South Vietnam during that month. By 1 July 1971 the VNAF still had only one gunship squadron, the number of assigned aircraft had declined to 16, and the squadron flew 23 percent of all fixed-wing gunship missions flown in South Vietnam during that month.[121/] (See Figure 20.) Although there were no additional squadrons activated during this period, training was underway for future activation. Thus the Improvement and Modernization program continued to make progress toward the CRIMP goal of two gunship squadrons.

Expansion

The second gunship squadron, equipped with AC-119G aircraft, was scheduled to activate in September 1971, and two AC-47 aircraft were to be added to the existing gunship squadron in August 1971.[122/] The 18 aircraft squadron was the most satisfactory size. That composition allowed elements of six to deploy: three for airborne alert, two for ground alert, and one for a spare.[123/]

VNAF AC-119 crews were integrated into the USAF 17th Special Operations Squadron (SOS) at Phan Rang AB in early 1971 for combat crew training. When the VNAF 819th squadron activated in September 1971, it would receive the AC-119Gs of the 17th SOS. Thus the VNAF trained in South Vietnam with an

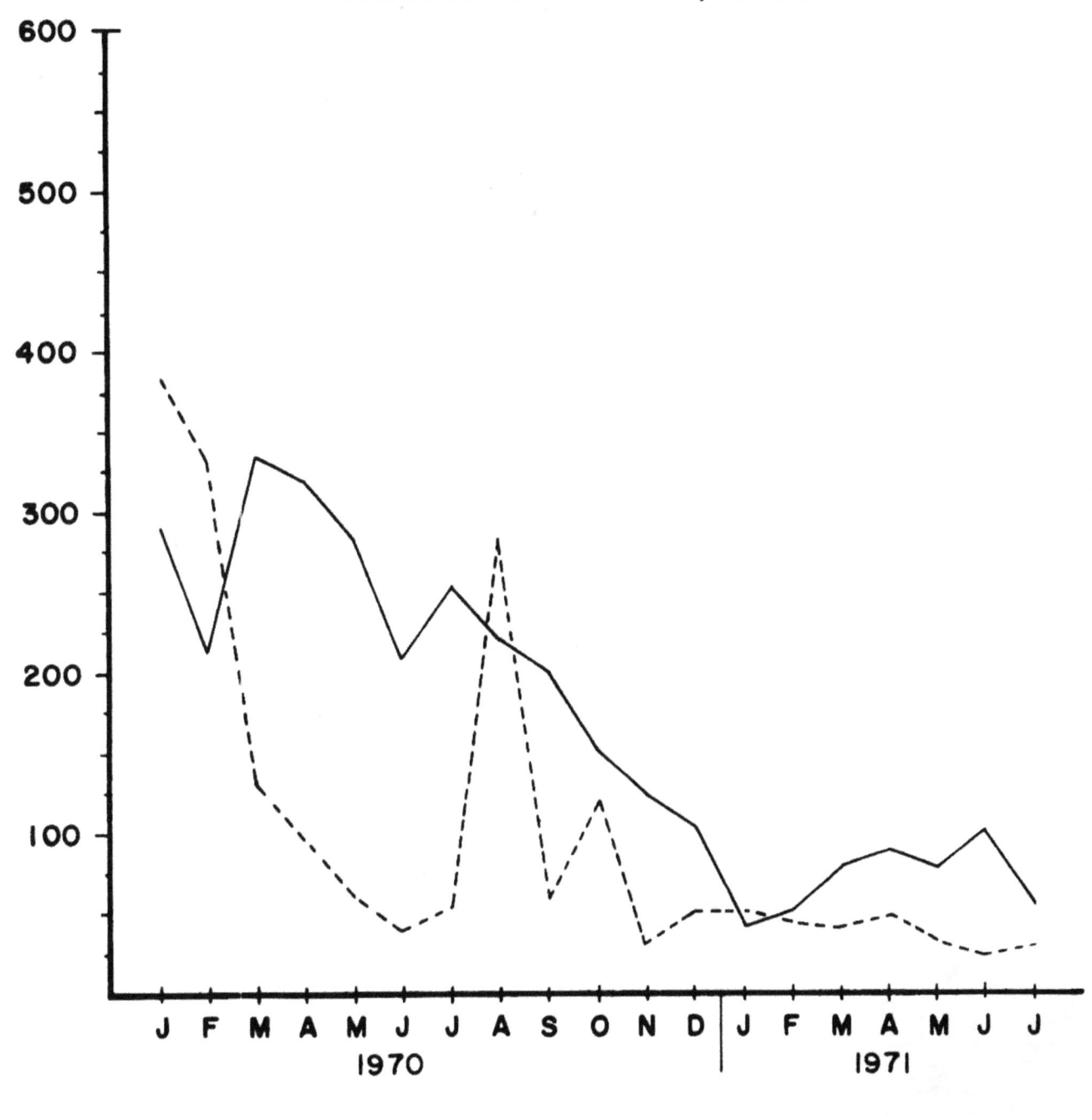

FIGURE 20

experienced USAF squadron and in the aircraft that would ultimately be transferred to the 819th squadron.* This integrated training program was remarkably successful.[124/]

In anticipation of the activation of the AC-119G squadron, the VNAF AC-47 squadron was to move from Tan Son Nhut AB to Nha Trang AB in August 1971. This transfer would increase gunship effectiveness nationwide since less flying time would be required for the gunship squadron at Nha Trang AB to support RVNAF units in MR 1 and MR 2. From Nha Trang AB and Tan Son Nhut AB the VNAF could effectively operate over all of South Vietnam and much of Cambodia.

The addition of AC-119Gs in September 1971 would more than double the effective firepower of the VNAF gunship force. Armed with four 7.62 mini-guns instead of the three carried on the AC-47, the AC-119G had a night observation sight (NOS) and a computerized fire control system. The AC-119G also flew faster than the AC-47. (See Figure 21.)

Maintenance on the AC-119G, like maintenance on the AC-47, was not expected to pose significantly new problems to the VNAF. VNAF transport squadrons were already equipped with C-119s and both the AC-119s and C-119s would be based at Tan Son Nhut, thus facilitating maintenance.

---

*For a thorough description of all gunship operations in Southeast Asia, both USAF and VNAF, see CHECO Report Fixed Wing Gunships in SEA, Jul 69-Jul 71.

With the activation of the AC-119Gs in September, the gunship portion of CRIMP would be achieved.

Interdiction

The VNAF, as conceived by CRIMP, was to have the capability to operate within South Vietnam, but not necessarily outside the Republic. Interdiction in Laos was not provided for in VNAF CRIMP authorizations despite the fact that the USAF had devoted considerable effort to interdicting the Ho Chi Minh Trail. Planners assumed that the USAF would retain this responsibility even though the VNAF gunships had an out-of-country interdiction capability. The continued presence and size of the residual USAF force came into doubt in mid-1971, however. During the same period, the Secretary of Defense called for a study on the feasibility of giving the VNAF a greater combat capability to meet threats existing or coming from outside its borders. Seventh Air Force undertook the study.

After considering three types of threats--overland infiltration from North Vietnam through Laos and Cambodia, air attack from the north, and waterborne infiltration--7AF planners concluded that the VNAF would have to confine its interdiction and defense to the borders of the country and that it could not carry out interdiction outside those borders. The study accepted the possibility, however, of "occasional limited forays into Laos or Cambodia," and did not consider VNAF options if later programs expanded the force beyond CRIMP.

When CRIMP was completed the VNAF would be able to deliver about 10,000 tons of ordnance with 6,000 attack sorties per month. While this

AC-119 Gunship

FIGURE 21

represented only about 20 percent of the U.S. interdiction effort outside Vietnam in early 1971, it approximated the support required by ARVN maneuver battalions in South Vietnam. The study assumed therefore that the regular army would occupy itself primarily with blocking the enemy in the border areas, while Regional and Popular Forces controlled the Viet Cong internal threat. In this case, the VNAF would support both, and make "random, generally small, independent attacks against lines of communications in Laos and Cambodia to harass and force greater efforts by infiltrators." Forward operating locations (FOLs) were to be used to support the ARVN near the border, although maintenance and supply capacity had thus far limited the VNAF to operating primarily from its seven main bases. [125/]

Summary

Thus the gunship force did not expand during this period, but the training required to reach the CRIMP goal of two gunship squadrons was proceeding on schedule. The role of VNAF gunships in interdicting outside of South Vietnam was also being investigated, but CRIMP planning did not provide for this mission in June 1971. If the VNAF assumed a larger responsibility for interdiction, CRIMP authorizations might have to be increased.

CHAPTER IX

AIRLIFT

In January 1970 the VNAF fixed-wing airlift force consisted of one squadron of 16 C-119s and one squadron of 16 C-47s. Of the 20 crews authorized for each of these squadrons, the C-119 squadron had 11 combat ready and the C-47 squadron had 12. Consequently, the C-119 squadron was rated C-3 and the C-47 squadron was rated C-2. (See Appendix IV.)

This rating, however, was not an accurate measure of the actual capability of the VNAF airlift force. Since the airlift squadrons were based at Tan Son Nhut AB, transport qualified crewmembers in staff positions at VNAF headquarters occasionally flew transport missions and thus augmented the number of crews available.

Expansion

No squadrons were added to the VNAF airlift force in 1970, but, in anticipation of squadrons to be added in 1971 and 1972, the 33rd Wing was reorganized on 11 January 1971 into the 5th AD with two transport wings, the 33rd and the 53rd. This reorganization resulted in some transport crewmembers assuming staff duties. [126]

In 1970 pilots were withdrawn from the C-119 squadron to train for the AC-119 squadron which was to be activated in September 1971. In addition, C-47 pilots were withdrawn in late 1970 and early 1971 for transition into the two C-123 squadrons which activated in May and June 1971. The forthcoming C-7 activations also drained qualified pilots from the C-47 and C-119 squadrons in 1971.[127/]

The addition of C-7s and jet-assisted C-123Ks would allow airlift operations into many short and previously inaccessible airstrips. The VNAF would thus be able to provide more effective support to ARVN staging areas and fire support bases.

By June 1972 the VNAF airlift force, as authorized by CRIMP, would grow from two types of aircraft to four, from 32 aircraft to 128, and from an average airlift capability of 126 tons per day in mid-1971 to 485 tons per day in mid-1972.[128/]

Training

The training required by this airlift expansion was staggering. The number of authorized aircrews would increase from 40 in 1970 to 180 by June 1972.* Additional crewmembers had to be trained to replace those withdrawn from the transport squadrons and assigned to gunships or staff duty.

The method used by VNAF planners to distribute rated personnel among the new units was to send C-119 aircraft commanders to the AC-119 squadron and C-47 first pilots to the C-123 squadrons. Aircraft commanders for C-7s were to come from C-47 and C-119 resources also. Copilots for

---

*The figure of 180 aircrews is based on the 1.25 ratio of crews to aircraft in effect in July 1971 as reflected by the July VNAF Status Review.

the new and old squadrons were recent graduates of pilot training courses in the United States. Many of the navigators for the new transport squadrons were graduates of the VNAF undergraduate navigation course which was established at Tan Son Nhut in 1970.[129/]

In an analysis of 5AD pilot resources prepared by AFAT-5 in March 1971, the shortage of aircraft commanders was identified as serious. Of the 242 staff and line aircraft commanders required, no more than 175 would be available by the end of the year--and that estimate was based on the assumption that every first pilot assigned in March 1971 (56) would upgrade to aircraft commander by December. Even so, only 70 percent of the required number of aircraft commanders would be available.[130/]

In addition to formidable aircrew training requirements, the growth of the 5th AD required maintenance training for the two new types of aircraft being delivered. New maintenance areas were also needed at crowded Tan Son Nhut AB.

MTTs were dispatched to Phan Rang AB during 1970-71 to conduct C-123 and C-7 maintenance training. Highly qualified VNAF maintenance men were trained by the teams and then integrated into the USAF 14th Special Operations Wing (SOW) where they instructed other VNAF maintenance personnel as part of an integrated training program. Aircrews were also integrated with the 315 TAW for combat qualification in the C-123. With the exception of the first 16 crews, all C-7 aircrew training will be conducted at Phan Rang also.[131/]

52

C-7 Transport

Figure 22

The transfer of aircrew and maintenance training for the C-123s and C-7s from the United States to South Vietnam was one of the most encouraging developments in the entire Improvement and Modernization program. This transfer of training built confidence in VNAF ability to become self-sufficient, and it saved approximately $800,000. But perhaps the most important result was the expected achievement of operational ready status several months earlier than would have been possible if the training had been conducted in the United States.[132/]

Performance

Even though the demands of expansion and training were great during 1970 and 1971, the VNAF transport squadrons continued to provide a substantial portion of the airlift support of the RVNAF. (See Figure 23.)

During 1970 VNAF transports carried 39 1/2 percent of the RVNAF cargo. During the first six months of 1971 the VNAF percentage dropped to 38, but with the activation of one C-123 squadron in May and another in July, the monthly percentage rose steadily, reaching 68 percent in July. Troop transport reflected a similar trend for both years.

Approximately 25 percent of VNAF airlift during 1971 was devoted to Cambodian operations, and many of the 1970 missions were also.[133/] Operation Eagle Jump, for example, in December 1970, supported ARVN operations in the vicinity of Kompong Cham airport. The operation was judged highly successful, but there was some confusion resulting from inadequate command and control facilities. To correct this, efforts were underway in 1971 to improve airlift communications and to train a combat control team.[134/]

During operation Eagle Jump in December 1970 and operation Lam Son 719 in March and April 1971, VNAF airlift forces demonstrated a surge capability. Operational sorties for December 1970 increased by nearly 200 over the average for September, October, and November of that year. In March and April, the number of sorties surged to approximately 150 more than the number flown in January and February 1971. (See Figure 24.)

In July 1971 self-sufficiency for VNAF fixed-wing airlift forces seemed imminent.[135/] The equipment and training provided by CRIMP as well as the continuing assistance provided by the Advisory Group was achieving results. In 1970 the VNAF airlift force carried over 30 percent of the troops and cargo required by the RVNAF. That capability was to be more than tripled by July 1972. An in-country maintenance training capability was being developed for both the C-123 and the C-7, and crew transition training for both aircraft would be established in South Vietnam before the end of the year. Although the existing pilot shortage was forecast to continue, a demonstrated surge capability was hard evidence that the VNAF could generally provide transport aircrew when necessary.

The most serious constraints was a lack of facilities at Tan Son Nhut. As one AFAT-5 advisor put it, the "USAF is going to have to downgrade its capability [at Tan Son Nhut] before the VNAF can upgrade theirs. The facilities--buildings, ramp space, etc.--are just not adequate for us to have an overlap."[136/]

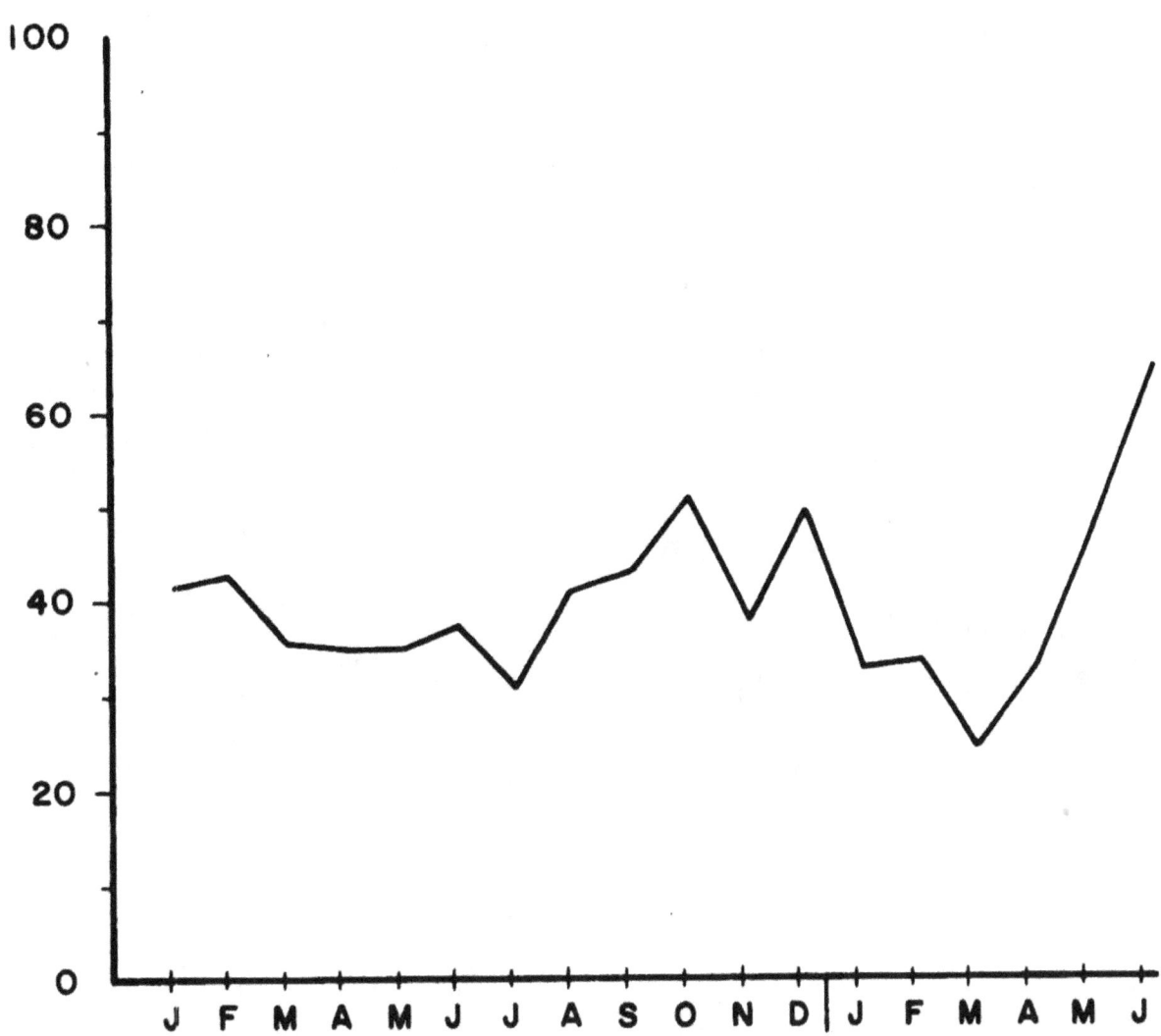

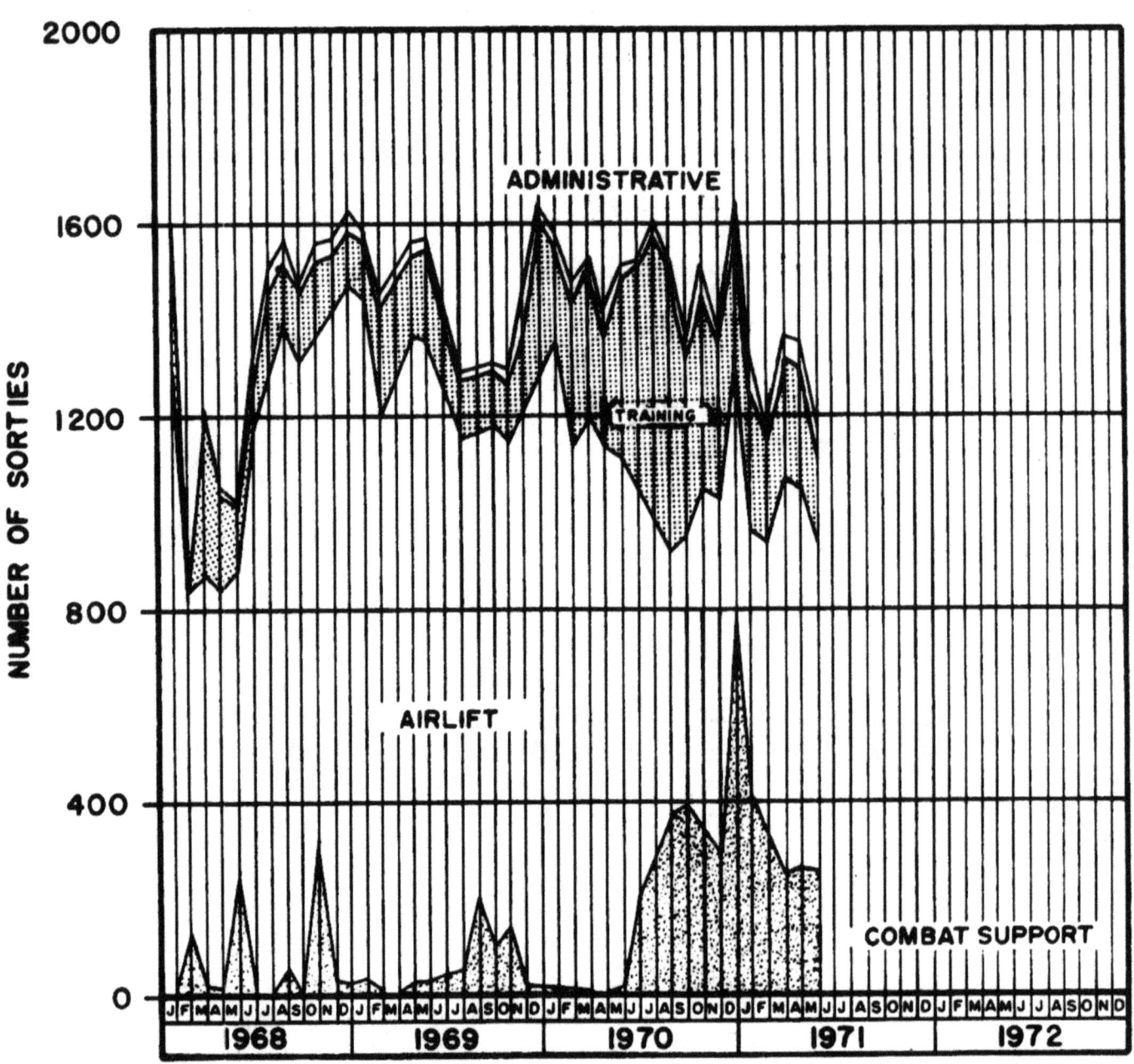

FIGURE 24

CHAPTER X

RECONNAISSANCE AND PSYCHOLOGICAL WARFARE

In both the VNAF and the Advisory Group, reconnaissance and psychological warfare operations received lower priority than other flight missions. Both missions were largely performed by the USAF during 1970 and 1971, and VNAF capability was not scheduled to increase significantly under CRIMP until 1972 when 20 EC-47s and nine RC-47s were to be added to the force. Six RF-5s were added in 1970 under Program II.

Reconnaissance

The VNAF reconnaissance mission was performed by six RF-5s stationed at Bien Hoa AB and by three RC-47s stationed at Tan Son Nhut AB. This force, according to an earlier CHECO report, flew only about 4 percent of the photo reconnaissance missions required in South Vietnam in early 1970. [137/] In January of that year the USAF flew more than 900 photo reconnaissance missions, but by June 1971 the number had steadily decreased and only 168 USAF missions were flown. [138/] Throughout this 18 month period the VNAF flew approximately 60 photo reconnaissance missions per month. [139/] By July 1971 most of the RVNAF generated photo reconnaissance missions in MR 3 and MR 4 were flown by the VNAF even though the RF-5 camera system, a significant portion of VNAF capability, had proven unsatisfactory. [140/]

The existing RF-5 camera system did not provide adequate area coverage and the AFGP Directorate of Operations (DO) recommended that a KA-56 low altitude panoramic camera and a KA-55 high altitude panoramic camera be installed. If a new camera could not be installed in the RF-5, the DO recommended that a new aircraft be acquired.[141/]

The addition of nine RC-47s, scheduled for 1972, would quadruple the number of those aircraft possessed and would significantly enhance VNAF photo reconnaissance capability.

In May 1970 a VNAF Photo Exploitation Center (PEC) was activated and integrated with the 12th Reconnaissance Intelligence Technical Squadron (RITS) for training. The VNAF PEC was declared operationally ready in September 1970, four months ahead of schedule, and by October it was judged ". . . self-sufficient."[142/] The PEC received a Texas printer (a rapid enlarger and printer) in December for processing 70mm film used in RF-5 cameras. Seven VNAF photo interpreters were trained in the 12th RITS Integrated Training Program.

In addition to photo reconnaissance, the glass bottomed RC-47s were used for visual reconnaissance of the Vietnamese coast. Vietnamese Navy observers flew on these missions with VNAF aircrews. Suspicious water craft were reported to naval patrol boats for closer examination.[143/]

Airborne Radio Direction Finding

The VNAF airborne radio direction finding (ARDF) mission was performed by U-6 aircraft in 1970 and 1971. CRIMP provided for 24 EC-47s by 1972. These would replace the U-6s and give the VNAF an all-weather multiple-signal capability.[144/] In 1971 VNAF ARDF equipment operators were to be

Integrated Training at the 12th Reconnaissance
Intelligence Technical Squadron

Figure 25

integrated into the USAF EC-47 squadron at Tan Son Nhut for training.

The substitution of EC-47s for U-6s would provide a more suitable aircraft for the ARDF mission and one that the VNAF was already capable of supporting. This would facilitate both maintenance and crew training.

Psychological Warfare

The VNAF psychological warfare (PSYWAR) mission was to disseminate propaganda by airdropping leaflets and flying speaker equipped aircraft for voice communications. The goal of the PSYWAR mission was to influence the opinions, emotions, attitudes and behavior of hostile groups ". . . in such a way as to support the achievement of national objectives." [145]

VNAF U-6s and U-17s were used to perform the PSYWAR mission. Effectiveness was limited, however, due to a shortage of speaker-equipped aircraft. Thirteen U-17s and one U-6 were equipped with speakers. To increase effectiveness, VNAF Headquarters directed in January 1971 that 95 percent of the allocated flying time for speaker equipped aircraft be flown in support of the PSYWAR mission. Support missions were to be flown in aircraft that were not equipped with speakers. At the same time, the VNAF and the Advisory Group prepared a request for two C-47s equipped with speakers. [146]

Leaflet drops were also part of the PSYWAR mission. Between November 1969 and September 1970, the aircraft of the 716th Reconnaissance Squadron dropped 125 million leaflets and transport aircraft of the 33rd wing at Tan Son Nhut AB dropped an additional 18 million. [147]

By July 1971 the reconnaissance and PSYWAR capability of the VNAF had not yet received the full benefit of the improvement envisioned by CRIMP. By late 1972, however, the addition of 20 EC-47s and nine RC-47s would vastly increase that capability.

CHAPTER XI
AIR LOGISTICS

In 1970 and 1971 the VNAF experienced a major reorganization with the activation of five air divisions. One facet of that reorganization was the expansion of the Air Logistics Wing at Bien Hoa AB into an Air Logistics Command (ALC) on the same command level as the Air Divisions. The thrust of reorganization throughout the VNAF was directed toward absorbing units programmed for activation as part of CRIMP, and toward more efficient management and effective employment of all Vietnamese air resources. To that end, the ALC was required to provide "depot level maintenance and logistics support for the entire VNAF force structure."[148]

"One of the Air Logistic Command's greatest needs in late 1969," according to an earlier CHECO Report, "was more training for its supply personnel."[149] That concern was shared by the Advisory Group and the VNAF, and in 1970 and 1971 considerable effort was devoted to training programs at ALC.

ALC acquired and occupied a new formal training compound in late 1970. The new facilities were a decided improvement, and included billets, classrooms, and a USAF dining hall. With the transfer of the dining hall to the VNAF, students began receiving regular meals in the training area for the first time and morale and performance were measurably improved.[150]

Training literature was ordered and received for all courses taught by ALC and over eighty 16mm films were also ordered. The literature was acquired from USAF Technical Training Centers and was in English; the films were to be made specifically for the ALC training program and would be in Vietnamese.

Formal training, OJT, ITP, and MTTs were all employed. In 1970, 454 students graduated from formal training and 1,883 were scheduled to graduate in 1971. Courses included metals processing, corrosion control, supply accounting, and other courses related to ALC functions, but students were drawn from the Air Divisions as well as ALC. Many of these courses would eventually be taught by ATC at Nha Trang AB, but until training facilities and instructors were available at Nha Trang, they would be taught by ALC personnel. [151]

Seven MTTs conducted courses at ALC in 1970 and 1971. Twenty depot personnel were trained as console operators for the UNIVAC 1050-II computer acquired by ALC in March 1970. Two MTTs helped establish depot level maintenance on communications systems in late 1970 and early 1971. [152] A supply MTT was scheduled to arrive at Bien Hoa AB in September to establish four new supply courses and to train VNAF instructors. [153]

During the first six months of 1971, 196 ALC airmen and NCOs upgraded to five level skills through OJT, and five airmen upgraded as a result of ITP. Another 29 received familiarization training through ITP. [154]

One member of the USAF Mobile Training Team at the VNAF Air Logistics Center giving instruction and assistance.

Figure 26

Thus, training at ALC was a significant feature of the I&M program. As a result, important progress was made toward self-sufficiency during this period.

The ALC had three major operational organizations with which to provide logistic support to the VNAF: A Material Management Center (MMC) a Maintenance Engineering Wing (MEW), and a Supply and Transportation Center (STC).[155/]

The MMC was the focal point for determining VNAF quantitative requirements and controlling reparable items. The major tool for performing this task was a UNIVAC 1050-II computer which was delivered to Bien Hoa AB in March 1970. Through the remainder of 1970 and the first half of 1971, a major goal of AFAT-6 was to train VNAF personnel to operate the computer and then to transfer the responsibility to them. The training was conducted by a MTT. By July 1971 responsibility for computer scheduling, downtime reporting, and utilization reporting were ". . . assumed completely by the VNAF due to their response to advisory training efforts."[156/]

In document processing, engine repair management, bench stock replenishment, and lateral coordination the VNAF became increasingly competent. Training was a vital factor promoting this trend, but perhaps the timely transfer of responsibility was the key. Both air forces were willing for the VNAF to assume responsibility at an early date. The transfer of responsibility for the Master Repair Schedule (MRS) from the

USAF to the VNAF is an example of this trend.

The MRS was negotiated quarterly between the MMC and the MEW. In these negotiations, MEW personnel forecast the man-hour capability of work centers as well as total MEW workload capabilities for the next eight quarters. Personnel from the MMC forecast requirements. Negotiation between MMC and MEW personnel then matched capabilities and requirements.[157/] The responsibility for these negotiations was transferred by the following sequence.[158/]

    a. 1st Quarter FY 71: The USAF Advisors negotiated and the VNAF observed.

    b. 2d Quarter FY 71: The USAF Advisors negotiated and the VNAF assisted.

    c. 3d Quarter FY 71: The VNAF negotiated and the USAF Advisors assisted.

    d. 4th Quarter FY 71: The VNAF negotiated and the USAF Advisors observed.

Thus training and transfer of responsibility were coordinated. At each stage progress was checked and the VNAF assumed successively greater responsibility.

The MEW was responsible for all VNAF crash and battle damage repair within its capability, IRAN (inspect and repair as necessary), depot level maintenance, and corrosion control. With the exception of the C-7, ALC was projected to have an 80 percent component repair capability on all VNAF aircraft by the last quarter of FY 72. (See Appendix IV.) During the first six months of 1971, twenty-four aircraft received IRAN, major repair, depot level maintenance, or corrosion control in ALC shops. During the same period in 1970 only 13 aircraft were processed.[159/]

The STC received, stored, issued, and shipped material for ALC. Between July 1970 when the UNIVAC 1050-II was "turned on" and July 1971 the capability of the supply and transportation center was increased from 400 to 2,000 line items per day. With the programmed construction of new facilities and the installation of a UNIVAC DCT 2000 (data communications terminal) in late 1972, ". . . the VNAF will be fully capable of processing all supplies requisitioned by the ALC in a timely manner."[160/]

At the end of his tour as Chief of the USAF Advisory Team at the VNAF ALC, Colonel Roy B. Skipper reflected that:[161/]

> *The ALC has made significant progress toward developing into a self-sufficient viable depot level logistics support organization. Full capability to support the total VNAF force structure can now be attained by early FY 74 as a result of recent USAF changes in role and mission concepts for development of the ALC. Primary and most important was the change from a "Big Base Supply" concept to a "depot" concept with full responsibility for control of total VNAF assets. Concurrent with this change was the recognition and decision to provide to the ALC an expanded computer capability with sufficient capacity to handle total program requirements. With the phaseout of USAF units at Bien Hoa Air Base in FY 72 and subsequent expansion and relocation of the major organizational elements, particularly the Maintenance Engineering Wing, the Air Logistics Command will be well on its way to true self-sufficiency.*

Progress toward self-sufficiency was also made in the Air Divisions. Maintenance functions were consolidated at dual wing bases into a single AD organization for greater efficiency. Base reparable processing centers were established at all bases by early 1971. A Spectrometric Oil Analysis Program (SOAP) was established at each AD, and improved local engine maintenance capability. The VNAF became self-sufficient in armament and air munitions supply and storage during this period as a result of advisory assistance at each base and training provided by the VNAF-operated schools at Tan Son Nhut AB. The VNAF had assumed the Explosive Ordnance Disposal (EOD) function at all joint and VNAF bases, except Tan Son Nhut and Da Nang, by early 1971. [162]

The ALC contributed to the air division's progress toward self-sufficiency through training. In an effort to expedite supply requests from the air divisions, ALC trained keypunch operators to be assigned to the air division maintenance wings and provided keypunch equipment for them to use. The earlier system of mailing written requests to ALC where they were transferred to keypunch cards was thus replaced with the faster and more accurate procedure of mailing cards. Further improvements in this process were expected as base supply accounts were satellited to the ALC computer in 1971 and 1972, and instead of mailing the cards, the information would be inserted into the computer at base level. [163]

One serious problem experienced by ALC during this period was the arrival of extensively cannibalized aircraft at Bien Hoa AB for IRAN and depot level maintenance. Some aircraft arrived ". . . with instruments

removed by cutting the wires rather than disconnecting them." [164/]
In these flagrant violations of logistic management, messages were sent to the organization owning the aircraft requesting that the removed equipment be sent to ALC immediately.

By mid-1971 VNAF air logistics capability had made significant progress toward self-sufficiency by virtue of the advisory efforts of the USAF, the equipment provided by the MAP, and the VNAF appreciation of the importance of logistic support for combat operations. Training and the timely transfer of responsibility were key factors in VNAF progress during this period.

CHAPTER XII

FACILITIES

The transfer of facilities from the USAF to the VNAF was behind schedule in mid-1971. (See Figure 26.) Although the transfers had been jointly planned by 7AF, the Advisory Group, and the VNAF, delays occurred. Often VNAF units were activated and in need of USAF buildings and maintenance areas before USAF units were withdrawn or relocated.[165/] In some cases the USAF units retained combat missions beyond the scheduled transfer date.

Delays were critical and threatened to slow the achievement of operational readiness by some VNAF units.[166/] Progress was noted in facilities transfer in 1970 after the 7AF commander emphasized the Vietnamization had a priority equal to the USAF combat mission, but the problem persisted. In 1971 the departing Chief of the Advisory Group pointed out that for the VNAF to become self-sufficient, "the all too prevalent view of 'let's take care of our U.S. troops first, then they (the VNAF) can have what's left' must be reversed for the more important gains associated with our national objective of making Vietnamization succeed."[167/] By July 1971 the VNAF had assumed control of only one base. Soc Trang AB was turned over to the VNAF on 4 November 1970 at a ceremony attended by the Secretary of the Air Force.

Hard Core Facility Transfer Summary, 30 June 1971

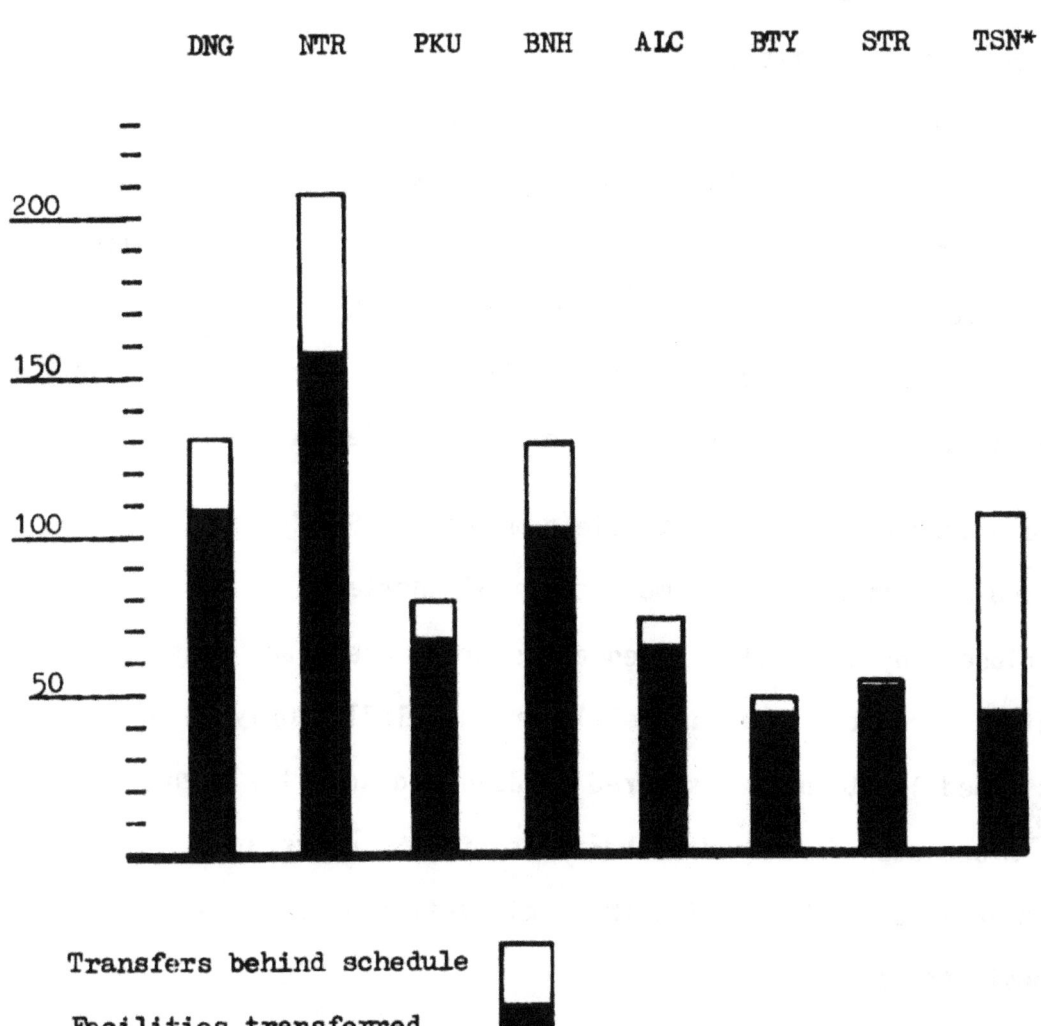

Transfers behind schedule ☐
Facilities transferred ■

Hard core facilities are those facilities that are mission essential.
*Abbreviations are explained in the glossary.

Source: Report: "Milestone Facility Chart," 30 June 1971, AFGP-XR.

FIGURE 27

The transfer of Soc Trang AB was marred by several subsequent events. Frequent power outages resulted from carelessness of inexperienced VNAF airmen, and the base water supply was exhausted on several occasions due to overpumping of low-yield wells. These and other incidents revealed that progress toward self-sufficiency in civil engineering and other related support functions had not been as rapid as in operational combat functions. Although civilian contractors in South Vietnam were employed to teach VNAF airmen the skills they still lacked to maintain a base, the training was not completed before Soc Trang was transferred to the VNAF.[168/] Lessons learned at Soc Trang AB were later used at Pleiku AB and maintenance training was incorporated more fully into the plan for transferring the base.

The most overcrowded base in South Vietnam was Tan Son Nhut AB. Maintenance space and billeting were the most critical shortages in 1971, but were followed closely by the lack of adequate storage areas and classrooms. Facility transfers were at a near standstill in July 1971. Only 45 of the 295 facilities scheduled to be transferred by July had actually been relinquished.[169/] Because of delayed withdrawals of U.S. units and accelerated activations of VNAF units, VNAF self-sufficiency at Tan Son Nhut was seriously threatened.

The VNAF billeting shortage at Tan Son Nhut AB was partially alleviated in May 1971 when one-third of a bachelor enlisted compound was transferred to the VNAF along with lockers, beds, and mattresses. Five hundred VNAF enlisted men moved into the 20 transferred buildings. A good rapport was established between the VNAF and the remaining USAF occupants, according to the AFGP. The other two-thirds of the compound was scheduled for transfer in September 1971.[170]

At Bien Hoa AB the shortage of facilities was compounded by the presence of both the VNAF Air Logistics Command and the Third Air Division. The consolidation of all USAF units on one side of the base helped alleviate the shortage of facilities.[171]

Conditions at Da Nang AB began to improve in early 1971. As United States Marine Corps (USMC) units were withdrawn, ARVN units assumed responsibility for defending the Da Nang area and USMC facilities on the base were transferred to the VNAF. At Nha Trang AB the United States Army began releasing facilities in late 1970.[172]

At all VNAF bases there was a serious shortage of dependent housing. It was so severe that MACV and the RVNAF Joint General Staff became concerned about the effect on morale. In an effort to correct this deficiency the United States agreed to provide equipment and material for the VNAF to construct family shelters. An austere ten-family structure was designed and approved. The cost was 600 dollars per family unit, and 4,900 units were to be built. Construction began in early 1971.[173] These dwellings were small and inadequate by United States standards. There was no indoor plumbing, but the roofs of the rectangular structures were constructed so rainwater ran off toward the open area in the center of the structure. Thus water could be collected, but many of the Vietnamese preferred to

VNAF Family Shelters Under Construction

Figure 28

enclose this area and add to the available living space. It was difficult to do this because water then tended to collect over the enclosed area.[174]

USAF engineers built the first shelters at each base as a model for the Vietnamese to follow. VNAF personnel, unskilled in construction, then joined the modest VNAF civil engineering staff at each base to complete the project. The first 10-family unit at Tan Son Nhut Air Base was completed on 19 March 1971. Only 20 percent of the work force were trained in construction.[175]

With USAF and VNAF interest focused on squadron activations and training for combat, the importance of transferring facilities on schedule was occasionally overlooked. When this happened, command interest was required to encourage timely transfers.

CHAPTER XIII

SUMMING UP

The goal of United States policy in South Vietnam during 1970 and 1971, as described in the Foreword to this report, was ". . . to assure the self-sufficiency of the Republic of Vietnam Armed Forces . . . after the withdrawal of United States combat forces." Self-sufficiency was defined as the ability to ". . . maintain the level of security that had been won jointly by the United States and South Vietnam."

VNAF progress toward these goals could be measured in 1971 by the growing number of qualified personnel and the increasing inventory of aircraft. This report has described that impressive growth throughout the VNAF during an 18-month period. For perspective, it is also instructive to take a larger view and compare the VNAF of 1971 with the VNAF of 1961--the year in which the USAF assumed an armed combat mission in Southeast Asia. In 1961 the VNAF had 70 aircraft and about 4,000 personnel. By July 1971, VNAF strength had increased to 46,660 personnel and 952 aircraft. 176/

There were other strong indications of growing VNAF self-sufficiency in addition to increasing numbers of aircraft and personnel. The USAF and the VNAF had jointly established a viable and effective VNAF formal training program in South Vietnam. American advisors judged the VNAF self-sufficient in training by mid-1971 except for pilot training and a few highly technical skills.

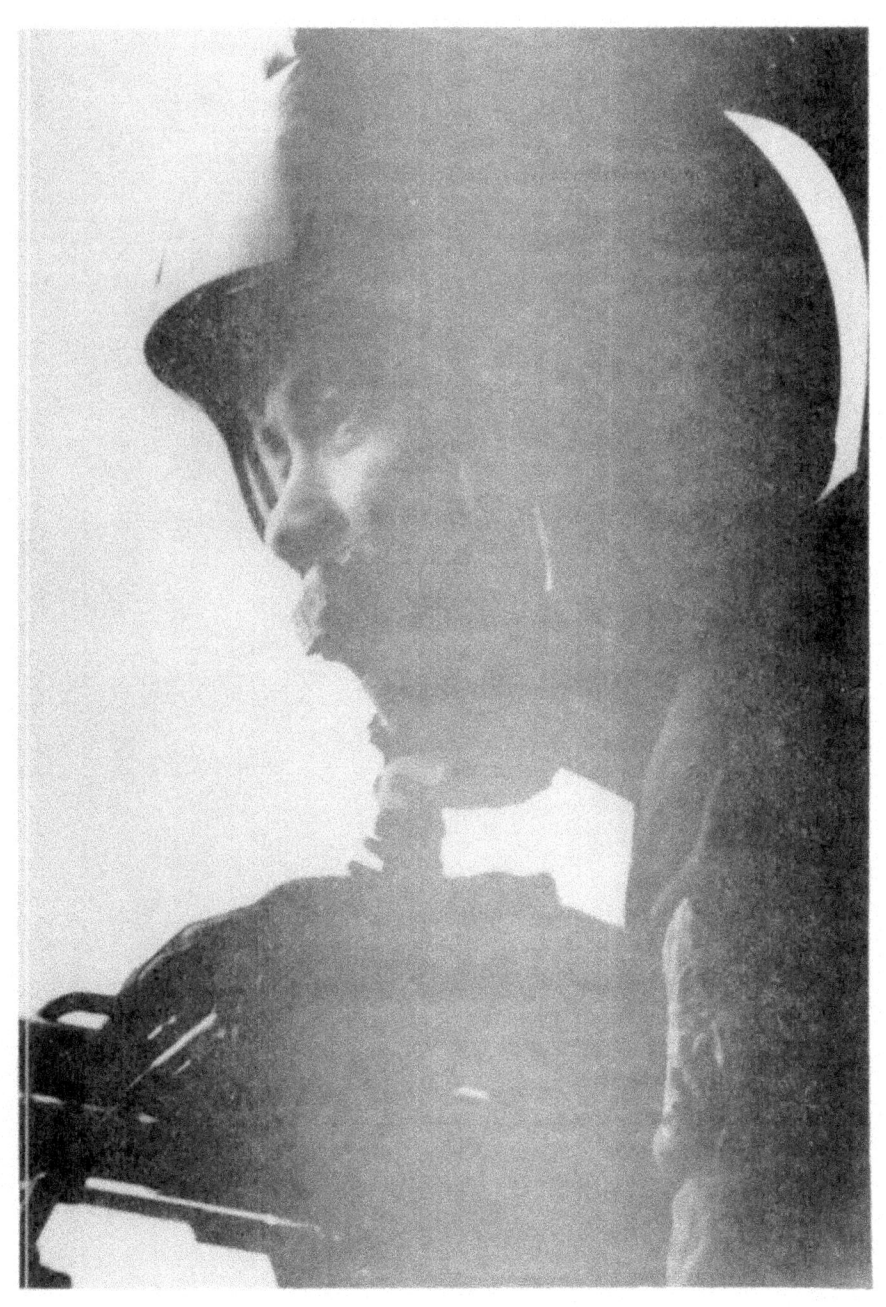

The Vietnamization of the Air War

Figure 29

VNAF maintenance capability showed a marked increase between January 1970 and June 1971. In January 83.5 percent of the 437 aircraft possessed by the VNAF were operationally ready; in June 1971, 75.5 percent of 873 possessed aircraft were operationally ready. The number of aircraft had doubled and five new models were added during this period. As newly trained VNAF maintenance personnel gained experience, the percentage of operationally ready aircraft was expected to increase. The Air Logistics Command also demonstrated a growing maintenance capability. Twice as many aircraft received IRON, major repair, depot level maintenance, or corrosion control in ALC shops in the first six months of 1971 as in the first six months of 1970.[177]

The evolution of a comprehensive doctrine for the employment of VNAF helicopters was further evidence of development toward self-sufficiency. The increased number of VNAF helicopters and crews was certainly a mark of the improvement and modernization achieved by 1971, but the doctrine for the employment of those helicopters--a doctrine developed and implemented by the VNAF and the JGS--was a more meaningful measure of the depth of RVNAF self-sufficiency. The United States could give the RVNAF the necessary equipment to defend South Vietnam but that would not assure self-sufficiency. In the final analysis, self-sufficiency would depend on the RVNAF developing the ability to effectively employ that equipment within the context of South Vietnam's military, political, and cultural ethos. The RVNAF helicopter doctrine indicated that the Vietnamese had the necessary ability. Furthermore, that helicopter doctrine indicated a Vietnamese initiative and willingness to make decisions.

The exercise of initiative within the VNAF, however, posed challenges. One of these concerned the influence accruing by virtue of VNAF reliance on the United States for supplies, and is described by an anecdote related by a Korean Air Force general. The general stated that in some instances it was useless for him to attempt to make decisions ". . . because he was like a beggar looking at a menu. It was all right to look, but he would eat what he was given." [178/] In other words, his freedom to make decisions about what he wanted or, for that matter, what he did not want, was limited by Korea's relationship to the United States. If he attempted to exercise his initiative by refusing what was offered, demanded something other than what was offered, or independently decided to what use he should put that which the United States gave him, he risked adversely influencing what he would receive in the future.

South Vietnam has a similar relationship to the United States. The exercise of initiative is therefore of less importance to the VNAF than the continued assurance of receiving military advice and assistance from the United States. [179/] The presence of major United States combat forces in South Vietnam exaggerated this relationship and encouraged the VNAF to rely on the United States to solve some problems (such as those faced in supply or base support) which might have better been solved by the Vietnamese themselves. [180/]

The disparity between American impetuosity and Asian patience also underlay many of the problems that were encountered during the improvement and modernization programs. One senior USAF commander who was closely associated with the I&M Program observed that: 181/

> *It has been a common experience in the aircrew training program to find that a student has an apparent lackadaisical attitude throughout the training. The instructor is quite certain that the student has a very small probability of successfully passing a tactical evaluation. Yet when the student is examined he is judged proficient in all respects. There is definite reason to conclude that as long as the instructor is present, some students expect the instructor to do all of the work. . . . Often the instructor will perform the task because it must be performed quickly or because he loses patience with the student.*

In operations as well as training there was occasionally a tendency to "lose patience with the student." When that happened the USAF performed the mission and the VNAF was spared the danger of serious defeat but denied the opportunity for significant success. Realization of the United States goal of RVNAF self-sufficiency would ultimately require VNAF exposure to the consequences of both. 182/

In mid-1971 the Vietnamese Air Force was rapidly approaching the strength goals authorized by CRIMP. But actual self-sufficiency would, in the long run, depend on United States policy and actions as well as Vietnamese strength.

APPENDIX I

VNAF FORCE PROGRAM

AS OF 30 APR 71

TYPE	UE	PRE CRIMP FORCE[1]		ADDITIVE FORCES								TOTAL FORCE FY 74	
				FY 71		FY 72		FY 73		FY 74			
		SQDN	UE	SQDN	UE	SQDN	UE	SQDN	UE	SQDN	UE	SQDN	UE
FIGHTER		<u>6</u>	<u>114</u>	<u>3</u>	<u>54</u>		<u>42</u>	<u>2</u>	<u>48</u>	<u>1</u>	<u>18</u>	<u>12</u>	<u>276</u>
A-1	18	1	18	1	18	(2)[2]	(36)[2]						
A-1	24	1	24			2	48	1	24			4	96
A-37	18	3	54	2	36	(5)[2]	(90)[2]						
A-37	24					5	120	1	24			6	144
F-5	18	1	18									1	18
INTL FTR (F-5E)	18									1	18	1	18
COMBAT (Gunship)		<u>1</u>	<u>16</u>			<u>1</u>	<u>20</u>					<u>2</u>	<u>36</u>
AC-47	16	1	16			(1)[2]	(16)[2]						
AC-47	18					1	18					1	18
AC-119	18					1	18					1	18
HELICOPTER		<u>5</u>	<u>149</u>	<u>9</u>	<u>264</u>	<u>4</u>	<u>115</u>					<u>18</u>	<u>528</u>
CH-47	16			1	16	1	16					2	32
H-34	25	1	25			(1)[2]	(25)[2]						
UH-1	31	4	124	8	248	4	124					16	496
LIAISON		<u>5</u>	<u>130</u>	<u>2</u>	<u>65</u>			<u>1</u>	<u>61</u>			<u>8</u>	<u>256</u>
O-1	10	1	10	(1)[2]	(10)[2]								
O-1/U-17	20/10	4	120	(4)[2]	(120)[2]								
O-1/U-17	20/5			5	125			(5)[2]	(125)[2]				
O-1/U-17	25/7			1	32			7	224			8	256
O-1/U-17	30/8			1	38			(1)[2]	(38)[2]				
RECONNAISSANCE		<u>1</u>	<u>12</u>		<u>6</u>			<u>1</u>	<u>29</u>			<u>2</u>	<u>47</u>
EC-47	20							1	20			1	20
EC-47	1		1										
RC-47	12	1	3						9			1	12
RF-5	6				6								6
U-6	8		8										8
TRANSPORT		<u>2</u>	<u>32</u>	<u>1</u>	<u>16</u>	<u>3</u>	<u>80</u>					<u>6</u>	<u>128</u>
C-7	24					2	48					2	48
C-47	16	1	16									1	16
C-119	16	1	16									1	16
C-123	16			1	16	(1)[2]	(16)[2]						
C-123	24					2	48					2	48
SPEC AIR MSN		<u>1</u>	<u>10</u>									<u>1</u>	<u>10</u>
VC-47	4		4										4
U-17	2	1	2									1	2
UH-1	4		4										4
TRAINING		<u>1</u>	<u>18</u>									<u>1</u>	<u>18</u>
T-41	18	1	18									1	18
TOTAL		22	481	15	405	8	257	4	138	1	18	50	1299
CUMULATIVE				37	886	45	1143	49	1281	50	1299		

[1] FY 70 and prior. CRIMP = Consolidated RVNAF Improvement and Modernization Program.
[2] Reallocations.

Source: <u>Action Officers' Data Book on Vietnamizing the War</u> (June 1971)

APPENDIX II

MOBILE TRAINING TEAMS

System	Training Location	Composition Off/Enl/Civ	Arr Date	Dep Date	Remarks
Navy A-1 (7-65)	Bien Hoa Tan Son Nhut	1/60/0	10 Apr 65		Provided training and guidance to VNAF maintenance personnel at Bien Hoa during its first month and then was reassigned to Tan Son Nhut on 15 May.
OSI	Tan Son Nhut	10	1 Sep 65	18 Dec 65	Conducted a course in OSI methods and procedures for 21 VNAF cadet officers.
H-34	Tan Son Nhut Binh Thuy Nha Trang Da Nang	6	18 Jan 66	26 Jun 66	Conducted H-34 maintenance training.
Management Survey	Tan Son Nhut Bien Hoa Nha Trang		11 Apr 66		Determined the quantitative and qualitative management training requirements of the VNAF.
OSI	Tan Son Nhut	4	25 Apr 66	1 Aug 66	Conducted two courses in "VIP Security" training.

SOURCE: Maillot, "End of Tour Report."

Course	Location	Students	Start	End	Description
Navy A-1 (8-66)	Binh Thuy	1/7/0	28 May 66		Taught VNAF personnel A-1 armament and maintenance procedures.
English Language Training	Nha Trang	4	1 Jan 66	19 Jun 66	Conducted English language training at the VNAF ATC.
AFIT Management Training	Bien Hoa Nha Trang Tan Son Nhut	2/0/1	24 Jul 66	15 Sep 66	Conducted an advanced management seminar for key VNAF officers.
F-5	Bien Hoa	1/10/1	3 Jan 67	Jun 67	Trained a total of 165 officers and enlisted maintenance personnel.
Logistics Management	Tan Son Nhut Nha Trang Bien Hoa Da Nang	4/0/0		Jun 67	Trained 76 VNAF supply and maintenance officers.
C-119G Maint	Tan Son Nhut		23 Oct 67	18 Mar 68	Trained 205 maintenance personnel.
C-119C Pilot	Tan Son Nhut		29 Jan 68	1 Mar 68	
Egress	Bien Hoa	6/2/0		15 May 68	Trained Egress specialists and personnel in parachute packing and survival equipment.
A-37 (7331)	Nha Trang		28 May 68	2 May 69	Maintenance training of 1,573 personnel.
OSI	Tan Son Nhut	6	6 July 69		Gave basic special investigation training.
(Project Seven Rivers)					
Command and Staff (8131)	Nha Trang	1/0/0	29 Oct 69	24 Apr 70	26 weeks. Assisted VNAF in organization of professional military education curriculum.

Course	Location	Students	Start	End	Description
Command and Staff (7436)	Nha Trang	3/0/0	5 Nov 69	1 May 70	Same as (8131).
T-41	Nha Trang	1/0/0	1 Apr 70	Before Aug 70	
XM-93 UH-1H Gunship	Binh Thuy	6/12/0	1 May 70	Before Aug 70	Trained 32 VNAF gunship crews.
Air Traffic Control (8113)	Nha Trang	0/2/0	1 Apr 70	2 Sep 70	22 weeks. Trained Air Traffic Controller and established course.
1050-II Console Operator (8134)	Bien Hoa	0/3/0	4 May 70	15 Jul 70	10 weeks. Trained 20 VNAF depot personnel as console operators for the U-1050-II computer.
RF-5 Pilot (7627)	Bien Hoa 3AD	1/0/0	1 Jul 70	16 Oct 70	15 weeks. Taught photo recon tactics and developed self-sufficient capability.
RF-5 Camera System (7628)	Bien Hoa 3AD	0/1/0	23 Jul 70	25 Aug 70	5 weeks. Taught VNAF personnel to operate and maintain the RF-5 KS-92 camera system.
EC-47 (8213A/B)	Tan Son Nhut	1/1/0	26 Jul 70	17 Sep 70	7 weeks. Trained two certification pilots and panel operators for flight facility check.
TACAN/Air-Ground (8189)	Binh Thuy Pleiku	0/2/0	1 Aug 70	1 Oct 70	8 weeks. Trained VNAF personnel in maintenance of AN/TRN-6 and GRA-34 monitors.
Communications Systems Maint (8202A)	Bien Hoa ALC	0/3/0	13 Sep 70	8 Dec 70	13 weeks. Helped to establish ALC depot echelon maintenance on new equipment assigned VNAF.

Distinguished Visitor Protection (7692)	Tan Son Nhut	4/0/0	12 Oct 70 27 Nov 70	6 weeks. Trained 81 personnel and developed an in-country capability for DVP.
Training Aids Development (8190)	Nha Trang ATC	0/0/2	29 Oct 70 19 Jan 71	12 weeks. Assisted in the establishment, organization and operation of the ATC training aids facility.
CH-47 (8232)	Bien Hoa	2/24/0	2 Oct 70 2 Mar 71	18 weeks. Trained 135 maintenance personnel in CH-47 equipment and procedures.
ABR Maintenance Courses (8087)	Nha Trang	1/54/0	7 Aug 70 7 May 71	40 weeks. To develop, monitor, and evaluate a total of 17 critical maintenance courses. There were two MTTs. The other one was designated 8196 and was composed of eight enlisted men.
Arbrn/Grnd Comm Sys Maint (8202B)	Bien Hoa	0/0/5	8 Jan 71 13 May 71	18 weeks. Trained maintenance personnel in depot overhaul at ALC.
C-123 (8239)	Tan Son Nhut	1/9/0	8 Jan 71 20 May 71	19 weeks. Provided familiarization training to maintenance, flight engineer and loadmaster personnel.
AMOC/A	Nha Trang	1/0/0	9 Jan 71 21 Apr 71	26 weeks. Establish an AMOC course. Assist instructors in preparing plans, aids, etc.
AMOC/B (8221)	Nha Trang	1/0/0	26 Mar 71 25 Sep 71	Same as above.
C-123/OJT (8247)	Tan Son Nhut	0/1/0	15 Jan 71 9 Apr 71	12 weeks. Provided assistance in developing an OJT program for C-123 maintenance personnel.

OSI (7273A)	Tan Son Nhut	3/0/0	25 Feb 71	18 Apr 71	7 weeks. Provided basic special investigation training to new members of VNAF Security Division and assisted in establishing a school.
OSI (7273B)	Tan Son Nhut	1/0/0	19 Mar 71	19 Apr 71	4 weeks. Same as above, but provided advanced training.
Dial Central Telephone Office (8248)	Nha Trang	0/5/0	24 Mar 71	22 Sep 71	26 weeks. Update the 36231 course and develop a 5-level course. Train 20 3-levels.
AC-119G (8250)	Phan Rang	0/6/0	15 Apr 71	22 Jul 71	14 weeks. Train AC-119 maintenance personnel, illuminator operators, NODs, MXU-470 gun system, radio and fire control personnel.
IPIS (8469)	Soc Trang Bien Hoa Binh Thuy Nha Trang Tan Son Nhut Pleiku Da Nang	4/0/0	1 Aug 71	30 Jan 72	26 weeks. Provide assistance in establishing and upgrading instrument training and flying proficiency programs.
1050-II Computer (8254)	Bien Hoa	1/7/0	1 Sep 71	29 Feb 72	26 weeks. Train 70 personnel in various supply AFSCs and basic Univac 1050-II training. Also evaluate and update six existing supply courses.
Altitude Chamber (8450)	Tan Son Nhut Tan	0/2/0	1 Dec 71	6 Apr 72	18 weeks. Assist in establishing and operating the chamber.

APPENDIX III

INTEGRATED TRAINING PROGRAM

VNAF PERSONNEL TRAINING IN 7AF UNITS

AFSC	TITLE	Officer Career Fields			
		COMP TNG IN JUN 1971	NO IN TNG ON 30 JUN 71	COMPLETED TNG SINCE 1 JAN 71	TOTAL TNG COMP SINCE 1 JAN 70
0046	DCS/MATERIEL	-	1	1	1
10XX	Pilot	14	51	14	14
14XX	Operations	1	-	1	1
15XX	Navigator	14	14	20	20
17XX	Weapons Controller	3	39	9	23
19XX	Safety	2	-	2	2
25XX	Air Traffic Control	-	48	7	41
30XX	Communications Elec	-	5	-	2
32XX	Acft Elec Maint	-	1	-	-
43XX	Acft Maint	-	1	4	4
46XX	Munitions	-	-	-	4
55XX	Civil Engineering	-	-	23	25
60XX	Transportation	-	-	-	2
63XX	Fuels	-	-	-	3
64XX	Supply	-	-	2	3
70XX	Administration	-	-	-	1
72XX	Political Warfare	-	-	-	5
73XX	Personnel	-	-	1	5
81XX	Security	-	1	-	6
92XX	Pharmacy	-	-	-	1
93XX	Aviation Surgeon	-	6	-	6
98XX	Dental	-	-	-	-
TOTAL		34	167	84	169

SOURCE: VNAF Status Review (June 1971)

APPENDIX III

INTEGRATED TRAINING PROGRAM

VNAF PERSONNEL TRAINING IN 7AF UNITS

Airmen Career Fields

AFSC		COMP TNG IN JUN 1971	NO IN TNG ON 30 JUN 71	COMPLETED TNG SINCE 1 JAN 71	TOTAL TNG COMP SINCE 1 JAN 70
20XX	Intelligence	-	-	2	4
22XX	Draftsman & Illustrator	1	-	59	59
23XXX	Photography	-	1	1	53
24XXX	Safety	-	2	2	4
25XXX	Weather	-	16	22	105
27XXX	Air Traffic Control	22	213	42	173
29XXX	Communications	6	49	41	64
30XXX	Communications Maint	7	119	50	135
32XXX	Auto Pilot	4	10	4	4
36XXX	Telephone & Wire Maint	24	80	73	134
40XXX	Intricate Equip	-	-	4	10
42XXX	Aircraft Accessories	5	6	25	47

APPENDIX IV

VNAF GROWTH, JANUARY 1970-JUNE 1971

TABLE 1

Helicopter Squadrons
January 1970

Unit	Type	UE	Aircraft Avg No Asgd	Avg No Poss	Avg No O/R	Auth	Aircrews Form	C/R	C-Rating
213th	UH-1	20	21.8	20.8	14.9	25	20	20	C-1
219th	H-34	25	25.0	24.4	16.3	32	26	26	C-2
215th	UH-1	20	20.8	18.8	14.5	25	21	21	C-1
211th	UH-1	20	27.6	23.3	17.7	25	20	20	C-1
217th	UH-1	20	26.9	24.6	18.0	25	23	23	C-1
Totals*		105	122.1	111.9	81.4	132	110	110	

*Four UH-1s assigned to the Special Air Mission Squadron are not included in the total.

SOURCE: VNAF Status Review (January 1970)

TABLE 2

Helicopter Squadrons
June 1971

	Unit	Type	UE	Aircraft Avg No Asgd	Avg No Poss	Avg No O/R	Auth	Aircrews Form	C/R	C-Rating
1st AD	213th	UH-1	31	33.3	30.7	20.9	39	40	20	C-2
	219th	H-34	25	28.0	23.5	17.2	31	26	25	C-2
	233rd	UH-1	31	33.2	33.2	21.6	39	41	19	C-3
2nd AD	215th	UH-1	31	34.0	30.0	24.5	39	38	38	C-1
	229th	UH-1	31	34.0	31.0	19.0	39	23	21	C-2
	235th	UH-1	31	33.2	31.9	23.3	39	12	10	C-4
3rd AD	221st	UH-1	31	34.0	33.0	23.2	39	26	26	C-2
	223rd	UH-1	31	34.0	32.0	22.5	39	40	32	C-1
	231st	UH-1	31	31.8	30.4	22.6	39	33	24	C-2
	237th	CH-47	16	15.1	15.1	9.8	20	25	25	C-2
4th AD	211th	UH-1	31	34.0	33.0	19.1	39	40	40	C-2
	217th	UH-1	31	33.7	31.7	19.2	39	33	33	C-2
	225th	UH-1	31	34.0	32.2	24.2	39	27	27	C-2
	227th	UH-1	31	33.1	32.1	22.9	39	25	25	C-2
Totals			413	445.4	419.8	290.0	519	429	365	

Squadrons to be Activated

243rd	UH-1	31	(1 Mar 72)
245th	UH-1	31	(1 Apr 72)
241st	CH-47	16	(1 May 72)
239th	UH-1	31	(1 Jun 72)

Total   109

GRAND TOTAL UE*   528

*The 219th Squadron is scheduled to exchange its 25 H-34s for 31 UH-1s in June 1972. Four UH-1s assigned to the Special Air Mission Squadron are not included in the total.

SOURCE: VNAF Status Review (June 1971)

TABLE 3

Fighter Squadrons
January 1970

| | | | Aircraft | | | Aircrews | | | |
| | | | Avg No | Avg No | Avg No | | | | |
Unit	Type	UE	Asgd	Poss	O/R	Auth	Form	C/R	C-Rating
516th	A-37	18	18.0	17.0	14.2	27	28	26	C-1
524th	A-37	18	18.0	18.0	14.6	27	32	30	C-1
520th	A-37	18	18.0	17.9	14.9	27	37	37	C-1
514th	A-1	24	31.7	28.8	26.4	36	35	35	C-1
518th	A-1	18	25.0	20.8	17.4	27	24	24	C-1
522nd	F-5	18	19.7	16.8	14.3	27	28	28	C-1
Totals		114	130.4	119.3	101.8	171	184	180	

SOURCE: VNAF Status Review (January 1970)

TABLE 4

Fighter Squadrons
June 1971

	Unit	Type	UE	Aircraft Avg No Asgd	Avg No Poss	Avg No O/R	Aircrews Auth	Form	C/R	C-Rating
1st AD	516th	A-37	18	18.0	18.0	12.0	27	16	14	C-2
	528th	A-37	18	20.0	20.0	16.7	27	13	10	C-3
2nd AD	524th	A-37	18	21.0	18.6	16.8	27	25	25	C-1
	530th	A-1	18	23.5	20.1	17.1	27	29	27	C-1
3rd AD	514th	A-1	24	25.0	22.1	19.8	36	26	24	C-2
	518th	A-1	18	22.0	15.0	13.0	27	21	20	C-2
	522nd	F-5	18	20.0	18.3	11.4	36	28	28	C-2
		RF-5	6	6.0	5.0	5.7				
4th AD	520th	A-37	18	20.0	17.6	15.7	27	21	21	C-2
	526th	A-37	18	20.0	20.0	15.8	27	19	18	C-2
Totals			174	195.5	174.7	144.0	261	198	187	

Squadrons to be Activated

1st AD	532nd	F-5E	18	(FY 1974)
3rd AD	536th	A-37	24	(Oct 1972)
2nd AD	534th	A-1	24	(Nov 1972)
Total			66	

Squadrons to be Augmented

1st AD	516th	A-37	+6	(Apr 1972)
	528th	A-37	+6	(May 1972)
2nd AD	524th	A-37	+6	(Jun 1972)
	530th	A-1	+6	(Jun 1972)
3rd AD	518th	A-1	+6	(Apr 1972)
4th AD	520th	A-37	+6	(May 1972)
	526th	A-37	+6	(Jun 1972)
Total			42	
GRAND TOTAL UE			282	

SOURCE: VNAF Status Review (June 1971)

TABLE 5

Gunship Squadrons
January 1970

Unit	Type	UE	Aircraft Avg No Asgd	Avg No Poss	Avg No O/R	Auth	Aircrews Form	C/R	C-Rating
817th	AC-47	16	18.0	17.0	16.4	24	22	22	C-1

TABLE 6

Gunship Squadrons
June 1971

Unit	Type	UE	Aircraft Avg No Asgd	Avg No Poss	Avg No O/R	Auth	Aircrews Form	C/R	C-Rating
817th	AC-47	16	16.0	14.7	13.0	24	24	24	C-1

Squadrons to be Activated

819th AC-119 18 (Sep 1971)

Squadrons to be Augmented

817th AC-47 +2 (Aug 1972)

GRAND TOTAL UE   36

SOURCE: VNAF Status Review (January 1970); (June 1971)

TABLE 7

Transport Squadrons
January 1970

			Aircraft			Aircrews			
Unit	Type	UE	Avg No Asgd	Avg No Poss	Avg No O/R	Auth	Form	C/R	C-Rating
413th	C-119	16	18.0	18.0	14.3	20	11	11	C-3
415th	C-47	16	22.0	21.0	19.1	20	12	12	C-2
Totals		32	40.0	39.0	33.4	40	23	23	

TABLE 8

Transport Squadrons
June 1971

			Aircraft			Aircrews			
Unit	Type	UE	Avg No Asgd	Avg No Poss	Avg No O/R	Auth	Form	C/R	C-Rating
413th	C-119	16	16.0	12.4	10.7	20	12	12	C-2
415th	C-47	16	20.0	18.0	15.2	20	17	15	C-1
421st	C-125	16	16.0	16.0	11.7	20	14	12	C-2
Totals		48	52.0	46.4	37.6	60	43	39	

Squadrons to be Activated

423rd	C-123	16	(Jul 1971)
417th	C-7	24	(May 1972)
419th	C-7	24	(Jun 1972)
Total		64	

Squadrons to be Augmented

421st	C-123	+8	(Oct 1971)
423rd	C-123	+8	(Oct 1971)
Total		16	
GRAND TOTAL UE		128	

SOURCE: <u>VNAF Status Review</u> (January 1970); (June 1971)

TABLE 9

Facility Transfer Summary 30 June 1971

	DNG	NTR	PLK	BNH	ALC	BTY	STR	TSN*	Totals
Total Facilities	414	452	430	740	346	391	278	426	3477
Total Hard Core**	167	208	114	130	120	57	52	93	941
Facilities Not Yet Transferred	136	112	180	72	161	136	8	264	1069
Hard Core Not Yet Transferred	62	51	47	29	58	15	2	51	315
Facilities Occupied By VNAF	282	336	250	668	179	254	264	163	2396
Hard Core Occupied by VNAF	109	154	67	101	62	42	49	43	627
Number Currently Late	33	87	30	24	13	6	2	186	381
Number Joint Use	10	6	36	7	12	18	0	11	100
Number Hard Core Late	21	50	11	26	8	4	1	72	193
Hard Core Joint Use	9	6	28	5	6	11	0	3	68
% Turned Over to VNAF	67	76	59	91	53	66	98	39	69

*Abbreviations are explained in the glossary.

**Hard core facilities are those facilities that are mission essential.

SOURCE: Report: "Milestone Facility Chart," 30 June 71, by AFGP-XR.

FOOTNOTES

CHAPTER I

1. (U) CHECO Report, *Organization, Mission and Growth of Vietnamese Air Force, 1949-1968* (Hq PACAF, 8 October 1968), p. 3.

2. (U) *Ibid.*, p. 4.

3. (U) CHECO Report, *VNAF Improvement and Modernization Program* (Hq PACAF, 5 February 1970), p. 5.

4. (S) CHECO Report, *Growth of the Vietnamese Air Force*, p. 7.

5. (U) Interview with Kenneth Sams, Chief, 7AF (DOAC), by James T. Bear, Tan Son Nhut AB, 22 April 1971.

6. (S) CHECO Report, *VNAF Improvement and Modernization*, p. 15.

7. (S) "End of Tour Report," Brigadier General Charles W. Carson, Jr., Chief, USAF Advisory Group, 5 August 1969.

CHAPTER II

8. (S) "Fact Book: Ambassador Bunker's Washington Consultations," Volume II, cited in CHECO manuscript by James T. Bear.

9. (S) "End of Tour Report," Brigadier General Kendall S. Young, Chief, USAF Advisory Group, 15 February 1971, p. 2.

10. (U) *Ibid.*, p. 3.

11. (S) *Ibid.*, p. 3.

12. (S) Briefing, "Planning for Vietnamization," 7AF (XRP), March 1971.

13. (U) Kenneth Sams, "How the South Vietnamese are Taking Over Their Own Air War," *Air Force Magazine*, April 1971, p. 30.

14. (S) Young, "End of Tour Report," p. 4.

15. (S) *Ibid.*, p. 4.

16. (U) Interview with Colonel J. F. Ballard, Air Force Advisory Group (XR), by James T. Bear, Tan Son Nhut AB, 30 April 1970.

17. (U) Briefing, "Planning for Vietnamization."

18. (S) Briefing Charts, "VNAF I and M," Air Force Advisory Group, 7 April 1971.

19. (U) Sams, "How the South Vietnamese are Taking Over Their Own Air War," p. 30.

20. (U) Young, "End of Tour Report," p. 9.

CHAPTER III

21. (C) <u>VNAF Status Review</u> (January 1970, February 1970, and June 1971).

22. (U) Interview with Major David MacIsaac, Major Nick Jones, Captain Jack Ferrell, and Captain David Schichtle, Air Force Advisory Group, Directorate of Training, by Captain Drue L. DeBerry, Tan Son Nhut AB, 15 September 1971. (Hereafter referred to as Directorate of Training Interview).

23. (U) Young, "End of Tour Report," p. 17.

24. (U) <u>Ibid.</u>, pp. 17-18.

25. (U) <u>Ibid</u>.

26. (U) Directorate of Training Interview; and
    (S) PACAF(XPXS) Ltr, subj: Project CHECO Rprt, "Vietnamization of the Air War, 1970-1971", 22 Nov 71. (Hereafter referred to as PACAF (XPXS) Ltr.)

27. (U) <u>Ibid</u>; and Interview with Captain The, (VNAF), Technical School Commander, Tan Son Nhut AB, by Captain Drue L. DeBerry, 3 Aug 71.

28. (U) Directorate of Training Interview; and
    (S) PACAF (XPXS) Ltr.

29. (U) "End of Tour Report," Colonel George E. Maillot, Air Force Advisory Group Director of Training, 15 June 1971, p. 11; and
    (S) PACAF (XPXS) Ltr.

30. (U) Directorate of Training Interview.

31. (U) <u>Ibid</u>.

32. (U) <u>Ibid</u>.

33. (U) <u>Ibid</u>; and
    (S) <u>PACAF</u> (XPXS) Ltr.

34. (U) Interview with Colonel Robert J. Heard, Air Force Advisory Group, Director of Training, by Captain Drue L. DeBerry, Tan Son Nhut AB, 30 August 1971; Maillot, "End of Tour Report," p. 11; and Young, "End of Tour Report," p. 18.

35. (U) Directorate of Training Interview; and
    (S) PACAF (XPXS) Ltr.

36. (U) Maillot, "End of Tour Report," p.13.

37. (U) Ibid., pp. 11-12.

38. (C) VNAF Status Review (January 1970), pp. D3-D4.

39. (U) Maillot, "End of Tour Report," p. 2.

40. (C) VNAF Status Review, (June 1971), pp. C3-C4.

41. (U) Directorate of Training Interview; and Letter, AFGP-XR to 7AF (DOAC), CHECO Report, Vietnamization of the Air War, 1970-1971, 15 Oct 71.

42. (S) Heard Interview.

43. (U) Directorate of Training Interview.

44. (U) Interview with Lt Colonel Osborne, AFAT-5 Advisor, by Captain Drue L. DeBerry, Tan Son Nhut AB, 5 August 1971; and
    (S) PACAF (XPXS) Ltr.

45. (U) Directorate of Training Interview; and
    (S) PACAF (XPXS) Ltr.

46. (U) Ibid.

47. (U) Ibid.

48. (U) Ibid.

CHAPTER IV

49. (U) News release number 3800, 7AF (OI), February 1971.

50. (U) Sams, "How the South Vietnamese are Taking Over Their Own Air War," p. 30.

51. (S) VNAF Status Review (June 1971), p. E-19; and Seventh Air Force Command Status Book (June 1971), p. B-4.

52. (S) VNAF Status Review (December 1970), p. G-37, (June 1971), p. E-19; Seventh Air Force Command Status Review (December 1970), p. B-7, and (June 1971), p. B-13.

53. (S) History of the U.S. Air Force Advisory Group, Military Assistance Command, Vietnam, 1 October - 31 December 1970 (AFGP, 4 February 1971), p. 43.

54. (S) Trends, Indicators, Analysis (Hq USAF), June 1970.

55. (U) Newsweek, 9 November 1970, p. 28.

56. (S) History of the Air Force Advisory Group, 1 October - 31 December 1970, p. 43.

57. (C) VNAF Status Review (January 1971), p. H-3.

58. (C) VNAF Status Review (June 1971), p. E-20.

59. (C) Letter, AFAT-1 (CH) to AFGP (CDE), "Summary of 1st AD Participation in Lam Son 719," 6 May 1971.

60. (C) Ibid.

61. (C) Ibid.

62. (C) Ibid.

63. (S) Interview with Colonel G. M. Howell, Director of DASC Victor, by John Dennison, DASC Victor, 3 March 1971.

64. (C) Letter, "Summary of 1st AD Participation in Lam Son 719."

65. (S) Interview with Captain F. C. Whitten, Hammer FAC, 20 TASS, by Major G. K. St. Clair, 8 March 1971.

66. (C) Hammer FAC Disum, 150.

67. (C) Ibid.

68. (U) Air Force Times, 26 May 1971, p. 21.

69. (S) Whitten Interview.

70. (S) Interview with Brigadier General F. C. Blesse, Hq 7AF, by Kenneth Sams, Tan Son Nhut AB, 11 March 1971.

71. (C) Letter, "Summary of 1st AD Participation in Lam Son 719."

72. (S) Howell Interview.

73. (C) Interview with Captain T. J. Calvanelli, Hammer FAC, 20 TASS, by Major G. K. St. Clair, 30 March 1971.

74. (C) Letter, "Summary of 1st AD Participation in Lam Son 719."

CHAPTER V

75. (S) Briefing notes, "VNAF Command and Control System Self-sufficiency," 7AF (DOCP), undated. (Hereafter cited as Briefing Notes.)

76. (C) "End of Tour Report," Colonel Franklin C. Davies, AFGP (DO), 6 July 1971, p. 26.

77. (U) Interview with Lt Colonel Tam (VNAF) by Captain Drue L. DeBerry, Tan Son Nhut AB, 20 August 1971.

78. (U) Ibid.

79. (C) Davies, "End of Tour Report," p. 26.

80. (C) Ibid., p. 27.

81. (S) Memo for the Record, subject: "Brief Description of VNAF Fighter Modus Operandi," Major Franklin P. Phillips, Chief AFGP Briefing Team [September 1969], CHECO Microfilm: S-380; 061.

82. (C) "VNAF TACS ALO/FAC Upgrading Plan," March 1969, p. B-5; and "Briefing Notes," p. 2.

83. (S) CHECO Report, VNAF Improvement and Modernization, p. 49.

84. (C) Letter, "Special Survey," from 7AF (IN) to 7AF (CS), 10 August 1971, p. 2.

85. (U) "Briefing Notes," p. 3.

86. (SNF) Letter, "Special Survey," p. 20.

87. (S) Memo for the Record, "VNAF Fighter Modus Operandi"; and "Briefing Notes," p. 3.

88. (U) "Briefing Notes," p. 2.

89. (U) <u>Ibid</u>., p. 8.

90. (C) Davies, "End of Tour Report," p. 6.

91. (C) "End of Tour Report," Colonel William A. Lafferty, AFGP (XR), 9 June 1971, pp. 14, 20.

92. (U) "Briefing Notes," p. 3.

93. (U) <u>Ibid</u>., p. 4.

94. (C) Davis, "End of Tour Report," p. 25; and "Briefing Notes," pp. 4-5.

95. (U) "Briefing Notes," pp. 5-6.

96. (U) <u>Ibid</u>., p. 5.

CHAPTER VI

97. (S) <u>VNAF Status Review</u> (January 1970, and July 1971).

98. (S) <u>Action Officers' Data Book on Vietnamizing the War</u> (OJCS, June 1971), p. B-45.1.

99. (S) <u>Summary of Air Operations</u> (CINCPAC, 12 July 1971), p. 18; and <u>VNAF Status Review</u> (June 1971), p. E-13.

100. (SNF) Young, "End of Tour Report," p. 40.

101. (CNF) <u>Ibid</u>., p. 40.

102. (C) Directive 310-19, "Directive on the Management and Employment of Helicopters," RVNAF J-3, JGS, 19 February 1971.

103. (C) <u>Ibid</u>., p. 5.

104. (C) <u>Ibid</u>., p. 11.

105. (C) <u>Ibid</u>., p. 14.

106. (C) Ibid., p. 23.

107. (S) CHECO Report, VNAF Improvement and Modernization, pp. 72-76.

CHAPTER VII

108. (S) VNAF Status Review (January 1970, and June 1971).

109. (S) VNAF Status Review (June 1971).

110. (U) Action Officer's Data Book on Vietnamizing the War (OJCS, June 1971), p. A-19.

111. (S) USAF Management Summary: Southeast Asia Review (20 July 1971), p. SEA-15.

112. (U) "U.S. Combat Role to End in June," Pacific Stars and Stripes, 20 September 1971.

113. (S) Seventh Air Force Command Status Review (June 1971), p. B-13; and USAF Management Summary: Southeast Asia Review (20 July 1971), pp. SEA 59, 61.

114. (C) VNAF Status Review (December 1970), p. D-8.

115. (C) Ibid., pp. C-14, C-15.

116. (C) Young, "End of Tour Report," p. 10.

117. (C) Ibid.; and Report, "Beacon Only Bombing System (BOBS)," AFGP-XR, 27 May 1971.

118. (C) Young, "End of Tour Report," p. 12.

119. (S) Study, "VNAF Role Against External Threats," 7AF-XPRW, no date, p. 3.

120. (S) Ibid.

CHAPTER VIII

121. (C) Southeast Asia Data Base Retrieval, Hq 7AF.

122. (S) VNAF Status Review (June 1971), p. B-2.

123. (S) Interview with Colonel J. H. Cronin, 7AF-XPR, by James T. Bear, Tan Son Nhut AB, 21 March 1971.

124. (U) Interview with Major Ronald T. Landman, AFAT-5, by Captain Drue L. DeBerry, Tan Son Nhut AB, 3 August 1971.

125. (S) Study, "VNAF Role Against External Threats," 7AF-XPW, no date.

CHAPTER IX

126. (C) "An Analysis of Rated Pilot Resources in the 5th Air Division (VNAF) for the Year 1971," AFAT-5, 14 March 1971.

127. (C) Ibid; and Landman Interview.

128. (C) Letter, "Special Survey," from 834th AD (C) to 7AF (CS), 5 August 1971, p. 6.

129. (C) Landman Interview.

130. (C) "An Analysis of Rated Pilot Resources," pp. 3-5.

131. (C) Landman Interview; and
     (S) PACAF (DOLOX) Ltr, Subj: Project CHECO Report, 19 Nov 71; and
     (S) PACAF (LGXX) Ltr, Subj: Project CHECO SEA Report, 22 Nov 71.

132. (C) Young, "End of Tour Report," p. 9; and AFAT Chief's Conference Discussion Item, "Feasibility of Conducting C-7 Aircrew Training In-Country," 17 January 1971.

133. (C) VNAF Status Review (December 1970, June 1970).

134. (S) Davies, "End of Tour Report," p. 11.

135. (C) Ibid, p. 2; and Letter, Proposed JTD Phasedown, AFAT-5, from AFGP-AFAT-5 to AFGP-CC, 17 March 1971.

136. (U) Landman Interview.

CHAPTER X

137. (S) CHECO Report, VNAF Improvement and Modernization, p. 93.

138. (S) Seventh Air Force Command Status Book (June 1971), p. B-3.

139. (C) Action Officers & Data Book on Vietnamizing the War (OJCS, June 1971), p. C-130.1.

140. (C) Davis, "End of Tour Report," pp. 9, 16.

141. (C) Ibid.

142. (C) "End of Tour Report," Colonel Senour Hunt, Chief, Air Force Advisory Team 5, 13 October 1970, p. 2.

143. (S) CHECO Report, <u>VNAF Improvement and Modernization</u>, p. 91.

144. (S) Cronin Interview.

145. (U) CHECO Report <u>SEA Glossary</u> 1961-1970 (Hq 7AF, 1 January 1970), p. 126.

146. (C) Davies, "End of Tour Report," p. 12.

147. (C) Hunt, "End of Tour Report," pp. 28, 29.

CHAPTER XI

148. (OUO) Air Logistics Command Plan 71-17, 30 June 1971, p. 1.

149. (S) CHECO Report, <u>VNAF Improvement and Modernization</u>, p. 103.

150. (U) "End of Tour Report," Colonel Roy B. Skipper, Chief, AFAT-6, 24 July 1971, p. 6-1.

151. (U) <u>Ibid.</u>

152. (U) Maillot, "End of Tour Report," pp. 23-26.

153. (U) Letter, "AFAT-6's End of Tour Report," from TN to CDE, dated 12 August 1971.

154. (U) Skipper, "End of Tour Report," p. 6-1.

155. (OUO) Air Logistics Command Plan 71-17, p. 1.

156. (U) Skipper, "End of Tour Report," p. 1A1.

157. (U) <u>Ibid.</u>, p. 1B1.

158. (U) <u>Ibid.</u>, p. 1A3.

159. (U) <u>Ibid.</u>, p. 1B1; and
    (S) PACAF (LGXX) Ltr, Subj: Project CHECO SEA Report, 22 Nov 71.

160. (U) Ibid.

161. (U) Ibid., p. 1.

162. (C) Young, "End of Tour Report," pp. 13-16; and
     (S) PACAF (LGXX) Ltr, Subj: Project CHECO SEA Report, 22 Nov 71.

163. (U) Skipper, "End of Tour Report," p. 1A1.

164. (U) Ibid., p. 1B7.

CHAPTER XII

165. (C) Briefing, AFGP to AFAT Chiefs, 1st Quarter 1971; Broadway Interview, pp. 9-10.

166. (C) Ibid.

167. (C) Young, "End of Tour Report," p. 41.

168. (U) History of the Air Force Advisory Group, 1 October - 31 December 1970, pp. 31-32; and
     (U) PACAF (DER) Ltr, Subj: Project CHECO Report, Vietnamization of the Air War, 1970-1971, 22 Nov 71.

169. (C) AFAT-5 Briefing Chart; and "5th Air Division Activation Progress," 5AD, 31 January 1971.

170. (U) History of the Air Force Advisory Group, 1 April - 30 June 1971, p. 14.

171. (C) Briefing AFGP to AFAT Chiefs, 1st Quarter 1971.

172. (S) History of the Air Force Advisory Group 1 January - 31 March 1971, p. 29.

173. (U) Young, "End of Tour Report," p. 26.

174. (U) Interview with Lt Colonel A. Lotterdell, AFAT-1 DCS/Support Advisor, by Major David H. Roe, Da Nang AB, 14 May 1971.

175. (U) Young, "End of Tour Report," p. 26.

CHAPTER XIII

176. (S) CHECO Report, Growth of the Vietnamese Air Force, pp. 19, 88, 89.

177. (S) VNAF Status Review (July 1971).

178. (C) Letter, "Special Survey," from Headquarters 14th Special Operations Wing (CC) to 7th AF (CS), 1 August 1971.

179. (C) Letter, "Special Survey," from Headquarters 625 1st Combat Support Group (CC) to 7AF (CS), 26 August 1971.

180. (C) Ibid.

181. (C) Ibid.

182. (C) Letter, "Special Survey," from Headquarters 14th Special Operations Wing (CC) to 7th AF (CS), 1 August 1971.

GLOSSARY

AB	Air Base
AC&W	Aircraft Control and Warning
AD	Air Division
AFGP	Air Force Advisory Group
AFLC	Air Force Logistics Command
ALC	Air Logistics Command
ALCC	Airlift Control Center
ALO	Air Liaison Officer
ALO/FAC-AGOS	Air Liaison Officer and Forward Air Controller Air Ground Operations School
AOC	Air Operations Command
ARDF	Airborne Radio Direction Finding
ARVN	Army of the Republic of Vietnam
BNH	Bien Hoa AB
BOBS	Beacon Only Bombing System
BTY	Binh Tuy AB
C&E	Communications and Electronics
C Ratings	A measure of unit combat capability determined by the number of operationally ready aircrews and aircraft available.
C-1	A high degree of relative effectivness. The unit is adequately manned, equipped, trained and capable of performing its primary mission: At least 85 percent authorized aircraft possessed, at least 71 percent of authorized aircraft operationally ready, at least 80 percent of

	authorized crew formed, at least 75 percent of authorized crews operationally ready, and at lease one operationally ready crew for each operationally ready aircraft.
C-2	A lesser degree of capability than C-1. Minor deficiencies exist in personnel, facilities, equipment, training, etc.: 61 to 84 percent of authorized aircraft possessed, 51 to 70 percent of authorized aircraft operationally ready, 56 to 79 percent of authorized crews formed, 51 to 74 percent of authorized crews operationally ready, and at least one operationally ready crew for each operationally ready aircraft.
C-3	A lesser degree of capability than C-2. Major deficiencies exist in personnel, facilities, equipment, training, etc.: 30 to 60 percent of authorized aircraft possessed, 25 to 50 percent of authorized aircraft operationally ready, 31 to 55 percent of authorized crews formed, 25 to 50 percent of authorized crews operationally ready, and at least one operationally ready crew for each operationally ready aircraft.
C-4	A very low degree of effectiveness. Unit is incapable of performing its operational mission. Extreme deficiencies exist in personnel, facilities, equipment, training, etc. Aircraft and aircrew readiness percentages are lower than those prescribed for C-3.
CRIMP	Consolidated Republic of Vietnam Armed Forces Improvement and Modernization Program
CY	Calendar Year
DASC	Direct Air Support Center
DNG	Da Nang AB
DO	Directorate of Operations
EOD	Explosive Ordnance Disposal

FAC	Forward Air Controller
FOL	Forward Operating Location
FY	Fiscal Year
GVN	Government of Vietnam
HPT	Helicopter Pilot Training
HQ	Headquarters
I&M	Improvement and Modernization
ITP	Integrated Training Program
JCS	Joint Chiefs of Staff
JGS	Joint General Staff
JPA	Job Performance Aid
LZ	Landing Zone
MACV	Military Assistance Command, Vietnam
MAP	Military Assistance Program
MEW	Maintenance Engineering Wing
mm	Millimeter
MMC	Material Management Center
MR	Military Region
MRS	Master Repair Schedule
MTTS	Mobile Training Teams

NOS	Night Observation Sight
NTR	Nha Trang AB
OJT	On-the-job Training
PEC	Photo Exploitation Center
PKU	Pleiku AB
PSYWAR	Psychological Warfare
Recce	Reconnaissance
RITS	Reconnaissance Intelligence Technical Squadron
RVNAF	Republic of Vietnam Armed Forces
SAC	Strategic Air Command
SAR	Search and Rescue
SOAP	Spectrometric Oil Analysis Program
SOS	Special Operations Squadron
SOW	Special Operations Wing
STC	Supply and Transportation Center
STR	Soc Trang AB
TACC	Tactical Air Control Center
TACP	Tactical Air Control Party
TACS	Tactical Air Control System
TOC	Tactical Operations Center

TSN	Tan Son Nhut AB
TUOC	Tactical Unit Operations Center
UPT	Undergraduate Pilot Training
USAF	United States Air Force
USMC	United States Marine Corps
VMC	Visual Meteorological Conditions
VNAF	Vietnamese Air Force
WG	Wing